Acclaim for

Unlock Your Educational Potential

✦ "This book is very practical and speaks directly to the many students who are working toward success in their educational endeavors. The advice is exceptionally well articulated, and the clarity of the language is wonderful. This book should become part of every student's tool kit."

— *Dr. Carolyn Kane, Professor, UC Berkeley*

✦ "Achieving academic success is a multifaceted challenge. *Unlock Your Educational Potential* addresses all of these factors in a comprehensive and understandable manner. It is an extremely valuable resource for achievement-oriented students looking to reach their maximum potential."

— *Bob and Debbie Graziano, Parents*

✦ "A great contribution to the educational community! This book is filled with timeless wisdom and powerful strategies that will make a positive and significant impact on students' lives."

—*Norma Lopez-Reid, Former Mayor, City of Montebello*

✦ "Supremely practical! Approaching success from many angles, the authors weave useful strategies into a blanket that covers all aspects of unlocking your educational potential. More importantly, the authors' passion for education is palpable and contagious. Students will benefit tremendously through application of these principles, and will continue advancing in school and life."

— *Michael Warren, Student*

✦ "*Unlock Your Educational Potential* is full of wonderful insights and strategies that will help students get the most out of their education. A must-read book for students and parents."

— *Fal Asrani, Principal, Corona Del Mar High School*

Unlock Your Educational Potential

✦ "*Unlock Your Educational Potential* is a valuable resource that demystifies the many unknowns that come with pursuing an education. It provides the tools and information necessary to achieve educational success. Students as well as their parents should read this book."

— *Maya Kelley, College Instructor / Counselor, Orange Coast College*

✦ "This book should be required reading for any student pursuing an education. The information is presented in a straightforward, enjoyable, and understandable format. I wish this valuable resource had been available when I was in school."

— *Helen Morgan, Director of State and Federal Categorical Programs, Hawthorne School District*

✦ "This book provides all the advice and wisdom you would want to give any student striving for educational success. It's filled with practical information that students can begin implementing in their lives immediately. The foundational principles set forth in this book set the stage for not only educational success, but lifelong success."

— *Dr. Russell Christensen, UCLA Professor*

✦ "I found this book very practical and useful. I could apply it to my own experience as both a student and an educator. I wish I had read this book earlier."

— *Jennifer Fan, Student and Educator*

✦ "*Unlock Your Educational Potential* is a must have for all students. The key ingredients to preparing for and succeeding in college are thoroughly explained in an interactive and easy-to-read manner. The book provides important information that most people wish they would have had before they went to college."

— *Frank Donavan, Administrator, Student Services, Westminster School District*

✦ "This book provides not only the ABC's of how to succeed in obtaining and enjoying an education, but it also provides the ABC's of how to achieve life successes through mental, physical and spiritual well-being. This is a must read for everyone."

— *Lorraine Dowling, Parent*

✦ "Brian and Jeff Haig have come up with a comprehensive source which will help students see, unlock and attain their educational potential."

—*Raymond R. Dunne, Principal, Santa Margarita Catholic High School*

✦ "Educators always make student success sound so easy. However, it's not that easy for students who don't know how to navigate through the educational system. This book is an important contribution to student achievement—it equips students with the knowledge of how to survive the educational environment and become successful."

— *Rebecca Botello, Director / College Instructor, Golden West College*

✦ "We highly recommend this book to any high school or college students who really want to make the most of their educational years. The strategies presented to succeed in and enjoy all aspects of school are time-tested and remain effective. True learning will take place on many levels and will spearhead students into life well prepared to develop and achieve their dreams."

— *Chris and Marjorie Trujillo, Parents*

Unlock Your Educational Potential

What Every Student Needs to Know to Succeed

Dr. Brian R. Haig

Jeffrey D. Haig

THF
PUBLISHING

Unlock Your Educational Potential
What Every Student Needs to Know to Succeed
Copyright © 2008 by Dr. Brian R. Haig, Jeffrey D. Haig

THF Publishing
4199 Campus Drive, Suite 550
Irvine, CA 92612
www.MaximizeYourEducation.com

Cover design by Sherry Stinson, Tyler Creative
Interior illustrations by Erin Kant and Shawn King
Project coordination by Cypress House

Publisher's Cataloging-in-Publication Data

Haig, Brian R.
   Unlock your educational potential : what every student needs to know to succeed / Brian R. Haig, Jeffrey D. Haig. -- 1st ed. -- Irvine, CA : THF Publishing, c2008.
      p. ; cm.
   ISBN: 978-0-9815659-2-7
   Includes index.
      1. Academic achievement--United States. 2. Study skills.
   3. Motivation in education. 4. Self-actualization (Psychology)
I. Haig, Jeffrey D. II. Title.
   BF724.3.M65 H35 2008   2008901429
   155.513--dc22 0810

Printed in United States of America

2   4   6   8   9   7   5   3   1

First edition

*To all the educators of the world who
enlighten, motivate, and inspire us.*

Contents

Preface

What if we told you that the vast majority of students who pursue an education never fully reach their true educational potential? What if we told you that during these very critical and important years, most students progress from one academic year to the next not really knowing how to make the educational system work for them, but instead graduate with a diploma that represents only a fraction of their true capabilities?

The academic years represent a key foundational time that sets the stage for long-term career and life success, and it is vitally important that students are equipped with the understanding and skills to be as effective as possible during these crucial educational years.

But how should students go about taking an active role in their education so that they can truly maximize their full potential? This book presents practical insights, real-world knowledge, and fundamental strategies that will change the very way students view their role in their educational journey. If we told you that we could transform how a student thinks, and more importantly, performs in the educational environment, would we have your attention?

We invite you to take this journey into the all-encompassing educational system where we present to you what you need to do to achieve not only educational success, but more importantly, your true capabilities and potential. The critical information presented in this book will give you a new way of thinking about your educational journey that can very well change your life!

Part I

An Overview

Understanding what an education means and what it can do for you is the first important step to unlocking your educational potential. Making it all happen is the next step. Unfortunately for many students, this next crucial step never happens. Somewhere, somehow, during their educational journey something happens and many students lose their motivation, lose their focus, or just plain settle for a standard that represents only a fraction of their true capabilities. And either consciously or subconsciously they know this and have accepted it!

Far too often students do not fully maximize their full educational potential during their critical, foundational years. And more importantly, they are not fully aware of the impact these developing years will have on the remainder of their lives. Attributes such as character, work ethic, motivation, ambition, and creativity are important qualities that students develop during their educational years, and a lackluster performance only helps contribute to an individual who ends up "cruising" through life on autopilot.

In this book, you will learn the key strategies and principles successful students use to ensure their success, despite a sometimes considerably compromised background. You will learn that it doesn't take a genius, a lot of money, the right school, or even a great family who will support you every step of the way to become successful in your educational journey. Sure, all of this helps, but what it ultimately comes down to is having the right mindset and taking the right action in your everyday pursuit to accomplish your educational goals.

Perhaps you've already experienced setbacks and difficulties in your education, and maybe you've even settled for a place that you know isn't representative of the "real you." What you've got to realize is that today is a new day, a new beginning, and if you want to take charge of your educational future, you've got to let go of any preconceived notions that you may have of yourself. It's time to stop settling for mediocrity and the barely-get-by attitude. It's time to unlock your educational potential!

Are you ready to take this journey with us? Are you ready to unlock your educational potential?

Chapter 1

WHY AN EDUCATION?

Let's begin this journey into your educational future by gaining insight into the simple question "Why an education?" Is it really worth all those years studying for tests, taking all those classes, completing all those homework assignments and term projects, and sometimes having to learn subjects that don't interest you? In addition, you have to drag yourself out of bed early each morning to make it to your morning classes. The list can go on and on. Why bother when you can spend your valuable time in more productive and enjoyable activities, right?

Haven't there been numerous success stories of high school and college dropouts who've become very successful in life without completing their education? To illustrate this point you need look no further than Bill Gates, Steve Jobs, and Michael Dell. And if you consider success from a financial standpoint and look at the 100 richest people in the world, you'll find that some of these individuals never completed much formal education.

So back to our question: "Why an education?" Why bother to spend so many years in the educational system when it certainly seems that other, more potentially viable, options are available? Except, of course, the law states that until a certain age, you must take part in an approved state-accredited educational program.

But let's imagine that there was no legal obligation to take part in any formal educational training. In fact, let's imagine that earning an education is something you could choose to do as simply as you would choose to join a club or organization. Let's also imagine that instead of spending all that time in the educational system, you engaged in activities of your choosing, perhaps playing on a local sports team, getting involved in a photography club, or hanging out at the beach, then playing video games all night on your computer. But around the age of sixteen, you would most likely have to start working to support yourself and your interests, so you would have to start looking for the kinds of jobs you could get without a high school diploma or college degree. In today's society, especially with the enormous growth of technology, one has to wonder what jobs are available to someone with no formal education. It seems that even the most mundane and repetitive jobs require a high school diploma at the very least. And to secure a job that promises genuine intellectual, creative, and financial potential requires more than that. To land the really interesting and fun jobs such as an astronaut, lawyer, or doctor, requires a minimum of a high school diploma and education well beyond.

Unless your parents have a job lined up for you, or you have a brilliant plan to start your own company, have done the research and figured out what products and/or services you want to sell, have worked out the marketing strategy, and have the financial resources to get your company off the ground, then like most people you'll have to make your own way in life. And without completing an education beyond high school, it's certain that making your own way will be much more challenging.

A Flash to the Past

To gain a better understanding and appreciation of learning and the educational process, you have to look no further than some of America's founding fathers. When you do this, you have to wonder why some of them, including George Washington and Thomas Jefferson, not only consistently advocated learning, but instilled the idea of formal educational training in this country by being the visionaries behind some of the first American universities, including George Washington University and The University of Virginia. And then there was Benjamin Franklin, one of America's most respected and best-known entrepreneurs, inventors, and humanitarians, who greatly improved the quality of American life with his many inventions, and also founded the famous University of Pennsylvania. He also founded the first public library.

Benjamin Franklin

Why did Franklin found the first public library in America? Because, during Colonial days, most Americans had limited access to books. Only the wealthy and the clergy had access to large collections. Realizing that the public was interested in the arts, sciences, economics, politics, and social issues, and that there was no single place they could go to increase their knowledge in these areas, Franklin and some of his buddies from a local philosophical organization pitched in money to start the first library so that everyone in the community could learn.

Why did these great early Americans place a huge emphasis on learning and the educational process? In fact, why were they so incredibly motivated about the idea of an education that they ultimately became the visionaries behind some of the first American universities that still exist to this day? By understanding this, you will begin to realize what an education really meant for these early colonizers, why an education was such a crucial part of their lives, and why it is such a crucial part of our functioning in society to this very day.

It is a well-known fact that the colonists placed great emphasis on learning because they believed that one could achieve "*freedom through education.*" Remember that in the 1700s, the colonists were oppressed by the British monarchy. Freedom of thought, of expression, and of choice was not fully possible, and to achieve a status where the human mind would not be suppressed, the colonists had to rebel against the British monarchy to create their own country. They believed that by continually trying to expand their minds through learning and by educating one another, they could gain "*freedom through education.*" And keep in mind this all occurred during the days when slavery existed, women's rights were nonexistent, and most of the people were illiterate — so this whole "*freedom through education*" concept obviously still had a long way to go. But certainly the roots of the successful and technologically advanced America that we know today came from the existence of organized educational institutions that allowed the teaching, and thus the learning of what was necessary for freedom and progress. This knowledge was passed on from generation to generation and enabled America to become what it is today.

And it is through this educational process that we as a society have become even more inspired to continue to learn, to create, and to innovate. Just think about what America and the rest of the world would be like if the simple concept of the book did not exist or if there were no schools or opportunities to learn. Our society would become stagnant, advancing at an unprecedented snail-like pace. Forget about checking your e-mail, surfing the Internet, calling your buddies on your cell phone, listening to music on your MP3 player, or any other such luxuries. Not to mention, medical technology would not be nearly as advanced as it is today, so if you were to get sick, just hope that the medication or surgical procedure you needed to recover would be available!

So let's get back to our original question: "Why an education?" Perhaps mentioning the hypothetical situation in which we imagined a world in which an education was not required didn't get you thinking. Or perhaps the facts about America's Founding Fathers and their "*freedom through education*" philosophy didn't inspire you. Or perhaps the idea that medical technology would revert to the Stone Age if there were no books didn't get you a little anxious. Okay, maybe what you need are just some solid facts relevant to today instead of scenarios and facts about founding fathers and people who lived ages ago to get you excited. Well, okay, let's move on to current times.

Current Times

There is something about current times that is quite interesting in regard to this whole education topic that we've been talking about.

It's interesting because when one looks around at the billboards, TV commercials, browses the Internet, or just reads the daily newspapers and sees the companies that are such a huge part of American life, the leaders and visionaries of those companies in almost every instance have some sort of formalized educational background—they really do. Just look for yourself! Let's take some of the big-name companies that dominate the landscape of American culture including EBay, America Online, Nike, Google, and The Walt Disney Company. The leaders of these companies all have one simple thing in common—a strong educational background.

For starters, have you heard of Meg Whitman? This powerhouse woman is none other than the president and CEO of EBay—that world-famous online garage sale place. It's basically an online marketplace that sells billions of dollars' worth of stuff every year! Meg received a Bachelor of Economics degree from Princeton University and a Master of Business Administration from Harvard Business School. Unbelievable background, huh?

And then there is Steve Case who led the pioneering effort of the whole online community by creating America Online, which many of you use to chat with your friends and to tap into the information super-highway. Like Meg Whitman, Case also earned a bachelor's degree, studying political science at Williams College in Massachusetts. After graduating he took on roles in various companies before spearheading America Online—eventually making it part of the largest media conglomerate in the world when he purchased Time Warner, Inc. That would make him the #1 guy in charge of everything from *Time* and *People* magazines, to the cable stations CNN and HBO, to Netscape Navigator, ICQ, MapQuest, and more! Unbelievable from a guy with a modest beginning studying political science in college. But we're not done yet!

If this hasn't gotten you excited yet, let's move on to something that might really get you moving—or should we say running—The Nike Company. Nike is one of the most competitive sports and fitness companies around, with a mission to bring inspiration and innovation to every athlete in the world. The CEO and founder of this company, Phil Knight, realized that no company existed that produced high-performance shoes, and thus the inspiration to create "Nike" came about. Knight graduated from Oregon University with a degree in journalism, but it was during his years at Stanford University in the MBA program that he became inspired to create a shoe company. He says the MBA program changed his way of thinking and ultimately it was what changed his life.

You might be asking, "What does all this have to do with me?" Well, let's get back to our original question: "Why an education?" If you look at some of the most successful people, the visionaries, the leaders, the people who create American culture, initiate change, and who ultimately set the stage for how the American people live on a day-to-day basis, there is no doubt that a strong educational background gave these people the foundational tools to succeed in life. You still don't believe us? Let's look at this further.

You've heard of Google, the world's largest online search engine and the #1 source people use to look up everything from daily news reports to stock quotes. Well, it was founded by Larry Page and Sergey Brin, two Stanford University graduate students — now billionaires because of their revolutionary idea! So what does it take to create a dynamic, revolutionary computer search engine that processes billions of random pieces of cyberspace information and makes it organized, universally accessible, and useful? It takes a collaboration of two minds with backgrounds in computer engineering, mathematics, and advanced concepts in theoretical computer science. Together, Page and Brin have earned bachelor's and master's degrees and credit toward doctorate degrees with emphasis in these areas, with more than a dozen publications in academic journals on subjects related to analyzing and extracting data from the Internet. Whoa, some heavy stuff here! But how much did their education contribute to their humongous success? You better believe, *a lot*!

But don't think that you need to earn all those degrees or go to a top school to accomplish success. Meet Robert Iger, the current president and CEO of one of the world's biggest entertainment companies — The Walt Disney Corporation. Iger graduated with a bachelor's degree from Ithaca College, and after graduation this mega-CEO worked as, believe it or not, a TV weatherman. However, it was his hard work ethic and sociable personality that moved him along his career path to finally run the empire of the Disney Corporation. He replaced Michael Eisner, who ran the company for twenty years. Eisner too was college educated. He graduated from Denison University where he studied English literature and theater. Something to think about.

It may be exciting to learn about all these hugely successful people who run these famous companies that are such a vital part of the American landscape, but you also might be thinking, *So what? What does this really have to do with me and my educational future? And what about all those other people, including those in the entertainment field or in sports — do they really need an education? What about them?*

The World of Entertainment

Have you heard of the movie *Superman?* We're not talking about the *Superman* from the early '80s, but about *Superman Returns*—the new movie. Well, that was directed by Bryan Singer, who also directed *X-Men*, *The Usual Suspects*, and many others. He began directing hit movies in his twenties. Do you think that a strong educational background contributed to his success as a director? Rather than answering this question, we'll let Singer, who graduated from the University of Southern California (USC) with a bachelor's degree in Critical Studies, answer for you. Singer stated that he is tremendously grateful for his time at USC because his major allowed him to better evaluate, interpret, and critique countless films. This ultimately allowed him to hone his skills as a director. A short while after graduating from USC he began directing those blockbuster mega-hit movies.

But let's check-in with an even bigger director, Steven Spielberg, and get his thoughts on an education. Spielberg recently graduated from California State University, Long Beach, after taking a thirty-three-year break from his studies. Spielberg, who initially completed three years at Long Beach State and then dropped out, finally returned to finish his degree because he believed in the importance of earning a college education. Spielberg, who's responsible for an unsurpassed number of mega hits, is considered one of the most influential directors of all time, and has won countless awards including Oscars, Emmys, and Golden Globes, was actually willing to set aside time from his hectic schedule to go back to school to finish his degree—now that is definitely something to think about!

While we're in the entertainment field, let's look at some well-known actors and television personalities. First, one of the most recognized women in America today not only graduated from college, but also continues to promote learning to this day. Yes, it is none other than Oprah Winfrey! Oprah attended Tennessee State University where she studied speech communication and performing arts, eventually earning a bachelor's degree. But she didn't stop there. She continues to promote learning through reading via her famous "Oprah's Book Club," a club dedicated to inspiring people to read. Oprah has recently opened a school in Africa for girls who don't have access to quality education, and plans to open more schools.

And then there are all those actors and authors who chose to pursue an education. Matthew McConaughey (University of Texas), Natalie Portman (Harvard University), Will Ferrell (USC), Angelina Jolie (New York University), and Jodie Foster (Yale University), to name a few, all chose to pursue an education. And famous writers including Stephen King (University of Maine), Dan Brown (Amherst College), author of *The Da Vinci Code*, and J. K. Rowling (Exeter University), who wrote the Harry Potter book series, all completed an education. Imagine the role education played in the success of each of these individuals. Certainly, their character development, depth of understanding, communication skills, confidence, and ability to comprehend and process information has been enhanced by their educational experience. How much this has contributed to their ability to function, behave, and perform in their daily activities and to succeed in their career endeavors, one can only guess. Undeniably, an education has given these people a greater ability to function effectively in society and has helped them to become more successful in their lives.

While we're still in the world of entertainment, how about imagining a scenario in which college-educated people are matched with those who are not college educated, to see who performs better. The match-up will involve the two groups facing off in various business-related tasks. These will test the ability of the individuals to use innovative thinking, to critically analyze and evaluate projects, to work with people of different backgrounds, and to effectively communicate and lead. Does this sound familiar? Well, if it does, it's because this scenario has already been played out on the hit TV show, *The Apprentice* with Donald Trump. And what are the results? Consistently, it was the college-educated candidates who came out on top in the tasks and who ultimately were hired by Trump to work on one of his business ventures in his hugely successful companies. It's quite interesting to see the results of a "head-on" challenge between "street smarts" and "book smarts" on *The Apprentice*.

What about the Athletes?

Even many athletes are jumping on the bandwagon of earning an education before ultimately pursuing their athletic endeavors on a full-time basis. Have you heard of the legendary John Elway? Elway is one of the best athletes in the history of football. Despite being drafted by both the professional football *and* baseball leagues during his years at Stanford University, he chose to finish his degree and play professionally only after he graduated. Though only delaying professional football for a brief period, Elway's legacy will be remembered as an athlete who broke NFL records, who was inducted in the NFL Hall of Fame, and who was one of the greatest football players in the history of the sport.

Then there's Troy Glaus, a professional baseball player with the St. Louis Cardinals. During his high school and college years, despite recruiting efforts by professional baseball teams, Glaus decided to complete his degree before going pro. Glaus not only earned a bachelor's degree from UCLA, but also helped win a World Series title and was chosen as the MVP (most valuable player) of the World Series!

And have you heard of Judy Foudy? If you are familiar with women's soccer, undoubtedly you have. This is because Foudy revolutionized the sport of women's soccer throughout America and the rest of the world by helping to catapult this sport into the world's spotlight during the 1996 Olympic Games when her team won the gold medal. And that's only one of two gold medals (she won the second in 2004). Foudy has earned countless other awards including two-time World Cup Champion. Despite the gold medals and worldwide recognition, Foudy also managed to complete her education at Stanford University, where she not only majored in biology, but also performed so well that she was accepted into Stanford Medical School. Ultimately, she decided that helping advance the sport of women's soccer and running soccer camps was what she wanted to do.

We could go on and on about countless stories from successful athletes who found an education an invaluable investment in their lives, but we think you get the point.

What do the College Dropouts Have to Say?

If you're not convinced yet that an education plays a crucial role in an individual's development and ultimate success in accomplishing lifelong goals, then let's take a look at some of the most successful college dropouts and get their views on this subject.

First, there is Bill Gates, who helped revolutionize the computer indus-try and is also one of the richest men in the world. Gates enrolled at Harvard University, but dropped out during his junior year to focus his efforts on Microsoft. Although Gates didn't complete his studies, in an interview on the Music Television Station (MTV) in 2005, he said that to get any decent job, you've got to go to college. If you stop after high school, you'll qualify only for repetitive, uninteresting jobs. High school is where you choose which track you're going down, and your choices in ninth grade will affect your entire life dramatically. Gates went on to say that it's education that has made this country so great, and it's really why we can call it a country of equal opportunity. He added that because the economy has changed, more people need to go on to higher edu-cation, whether community college, technical college, or a four-year university. Gates has received an honorary Ph.D. from Harvard.

And the times have definitely changed. What used to be an industri-alized society, driven largely by laborers producing goods in factories across the US, has now been transformed into the age of technology and information systems, where immediate access to information is readily available and Internet-based companies spring up practically overnight. So an education years ago wasn't an absolute necessity for success, but in today's technologically advanced society, you are going against the odds without a strong educational background. According to our former US President, Bill Clinton, "You are gambling with your life if you don't have an education."

Let's return to our successful college dropouts once again to get their viewpoint on this subject. You've already heard from the famous col-lege dropout Bill Gates, but did you know that he believes in an edu-cation so strongly that he created a foundation that donates billions of dollars to improve learning opportunities throughout the world? This money provides computer and information technology to academic institutions, helps create teacher training programs, funds academic grants for students, and funds a Global Libraries Program that increases access to technology for residents in low-income and disadvantaged communities. In short, this foundation's mission is to help all students graduate as strong citizens ready for college and work. Not bad for a college dropout.

Let's hear from two other very famous college dropouts—Michael Dell and Steve Jobs. Michael Dell is the pioneer of the concept of selling custom-built computers directly to customers without the added costs of the "middleman"—retail distributors. This novel concept turned out to be hugely successful, making his company, Dell Inc., one the most profitable PC manufacturers in the world. Originally a student at University of Texas, Dell had intentions of going to medical school; however, all that changed when the fledgling computer company he was running out of his dorm room started turning huge profits. Though Dell eventually dropped out of college to focus his energy on running his company, he later stated, "I was serious about college. I went to class and I did my work. And I would never advocate that young people today pass up an opportunity for higher education." Also, like Bill Gates, Dell believes in an education so strongly that he created the Michael and Susan Dell Foundation, with a vision to equip children with the skills and tools necessary to reach their full potential by graduating from high school and earning a college education. The foundation funds all kinds of educational programs, from mentoring and tutoring to awarding grants and scholarships to students. Again we find another famous college dropout who believes that students should stay in school and earn an education.

And then we have our last example of a famous college dropout—Steve Jobs, CEO and founder of Apple Computer and Pixar Animation Studios, two revolutionary and mega-successful companies. Jobs dropped out of Reed University after only six months of enrollment. Though a college dropout, Jobs, like the previous two college dropouts, has been a huge visionary and an advocate for education. He has created three different educational programs and has developed partnerships between Apple and schools in numerous communities. His efforts have led to millions of dollars worth of computers being donated to schools.

It's interesting that even the most successful college dropouts are promoting education. And you've got to wonder why everyone from the college dropouts to celebrities and athletes to famous business moguls has found an education to be an immensely valuable tool in life. Why is it that people from different backgrounds, with vastly different interests in life, have found such a common bond and value in the power of an education? Even to the extent that some were willing to forgo lucrative athletic and entertainment contracts, or promising business-related ventures, until they had completed their education. What is it about an education that has made it so appealing and worthwhile?

And to drive the point home a little further, it's not only the celebrities, athletes, business moguls, and college dropouts who have found an education to be invaluable, but also the felons—you know, those men and women sitting in prison. Many of them have come to the realization that a life of crime only brings a sad and empty existence, and that the key to a better future is through an education.

What better example than the story of the founder of the Crips, one of the most notorious street gangs in existence based in Los Angeles. The founder was Stanley "Tookie" Williams, who was executed by the State of California in December 2005 after sitting on death row for over two decades. Though he was involved in gang life during his early years, he later renounced his gang affiliation, apologized for having founded the Crips, and said the following about an education: "Strive to educate and discipline your mind… read every relevant book that you can get your hands on. Educate yourselves about history, world religions, math, English, spirituality, and your culture…. Learn about computer technology, politics, and the sciences." Finally, Stanley compared modern-day slavery to those who choose not to educate themselves. He stated, "A modern-day slave will neglect to educate himself, which in turn creates mental slavery. These days, everyone should take advantage of the opportunity to get an education."

Keep in mind that this is being said by the founder of one of the most notorious street gangs still in existence to this day and by someone who was on death row for over two decades! I'm not sure if we can come up with a more eye-opening example of how universally accepted the value of an education has become, and how its importance has resonated with every type of person imaginable—from athletes, business moguls, movie celebrities, and college dropouts, to even the felons (even the ones on death row)! So back to our question: "What is it about an education that has made it so appealing and worthwhile?" Why have so many people of such extremely different backgrounds and interests been able to find such a common bond and value in an education?

While the answer to this question is personal and unique to each person, there are some universally recognized answers that can shed light on what an education can do for you. An education gives you the ability to think at a deeper and more complex level. This will enable you to make more informed and educated decisions about anything that you do in your life, whether career- or personal-related.

Becoming educated will enable you to write more proficiently and read more intelligently so you can communicate more effectively and better understand the world you live in. This will have profound implications for your ability to succeed in life, and will help you fully appreciate the development of human relationships through communication.

Your pursuit of an education will expose you to culture and the arts. This will allow you to better understand and appreciate the differences among people's ethnic and sociological backgrounds, along with their unique abilities and talents for creating great works of art. It will also help you to understand yourself and your talents, and how those talents are meant to share your uniqueness and beauty with the world.

An education also reveals the value of history and enhances your understanding of your personal roots and those of your ancestors, along with how the world evolved and came to be. This can give you a deeper passion and appreciation for life and a stronger realization of your personal beliefs, interests, and philosophical values.

Moreover, an education provides a greater understanding of the sciences and of how technological advances throughout the ages have contributed to a more advanced, prosperous, and healthier society. Politics shows you how the interaction among governments has contributed to the rise, stability, and destabilization of nations. This will help you to understand world policy and reform and how the progress of nations in a multiethnic, cultural, and religious world has led to the need for better understanding, appreciation, and respect for individual differences.

And all this is just the beginning. Through an education, you are able to expand your mind and free yourself from mental imprisonment. Without knowledge, you will have an obstructed and very limited view of the world you live in. Knowledge is power, and with it you are given the possibilities to unlock your full potential—a potential that brings new hope and opportunities for growth and a brighter future.

On many university diplomas it reads, "Let there be light." This is because it is only through knowledge that you are turned away from the darkness into the light of truth, prosperity, and fulfillment.

ACTION STEPS

❏ Think about what an education means, and more importantly, what it can do for you. What would your life be like without an education?

❏ Think about why everyone including business moguls, celebrities, athletes, and even college dropouts has found a common bond in the value of an education. List three reasons why you feel earning an education has been universally accepted as a powerful way to succeed in life.

❏ Is an education important to you? On a scale of 1–10, 10 being the most important, what value would you place on earning an education? List three ways earning an education can benefit your life.

Chapter 2

Exploring the Educational System

Understanding the importance of an education and what it can do for you is the beginning of unlocking your full educational potential. Taking the necessary steps to get the most out of your educational journey is the next step. To harness the power of what an education can really do for you, you must realize that there are many different components in the educational system that work in harmony with one purpose in mind—to give you the best education possible! Your school has a vast array of resources and opportunities waiting for you to discover. To truly maximize your full educational potential, it's important to learn what these resources and opportunities are, and more importantly, to understand how they serve as the foundational building blocks for getting the most out of your educational journey.

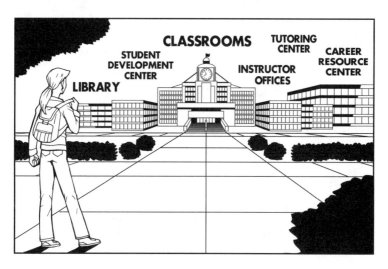

What resources and opportunities are we talking about? We're talking about everything that your school makes available to you including the student development office, tutoring center, career resource center and library, and the many different administrative and academic staff whose sole purpose is to help you get the most out of your education. There's also an abundance of teachers and mentors/counselors who are there to teach and guide you every step of the way along your educational journey.

You see, the educational system has been designed in such a way that every component of it serves as an integral part that works together to give you the best education possible. So you can be flattered by the fact that there is an entire infrastructure made up of many different academic buildings filled with many different people, including instructors and administrators, who are all there to help you. Therefore, the one thing you need to be clear about in your education is that you are not alone. There is a dynamic team of professionals whose primary job is to help you every step of the way to ensure your success.

Though your school has your best interests in mind, remember that it's up to you to seek out the resources and opportunities your school makes available to you and leverage them to your full advantage. The primary responsibility for your success, failure, or half-hearted effort to accomplish your educational goals ultimately lies only with you. Although you will have all you need to succeed, including instructors, administrators, and many different places that are available for assistance, realize it's up to you to be proactive and to develop the skills and habits that will allow you to succeed in your education.

Unfortunately, many students don't realize that there is an abundance of resources and opportunities available to them, or they don't know how to use them to their full potential. In this chapter, we'll show you the major resources and opportunities that are available at a typical educational institution. But more importantly, we'll show you how you can use them to get the most out of your education.

Succeeding in your education means that you must be aware of all the possibilities available to you. How else can you make the most informed decisions about your educational future every step of the way?

Begin with a Clear Plan

To succeed in your education you need a clear plan. As the saying goes, "If you fail to plan, you plan to fail." Without a clear plan of action, you might as well just wander around from one academic year to the next gambling that things will work out for you.

A clear plan of action means a decisive, step-by-step game plan that will enable you to get from where you are now to where you envision yourself in the future. For instance, a plan that will take you from your first year of high school or college to your graduation day with all your goals being met, whether they are to earn a specific grade-point average, to have taken part in certain clubs and organizations, or to have become involved in community outreach programs. It's up to you to be proactive and to take charge of your education, because although you may be getting advice from your parents, friends, or a guidance counselor, *the ultimate responsibility for your future lies with you.*

As an analogy, let's imagine you have a goal of trying to get your body into great physical shape. You want to improve your muscle definition, trim some body fat, and have a more toned, healthier body. To get that body, you have to go to the gym and possibly change your diet. But would you go to the gym and just start using random equipment to get the results you want? To get maximum results, you must know how to use the different pieces of equipment appropriately to exercise your body's different muscle groups. You must also eat healthy foods and in the correct portions. Finally, you must have a plan that will allow you to not only monitor your ongoing results, but also allow you to keep to a set daily workout regimen. Well, why wouldn't you want to take this same approach when pursuing your education—one of the most important endeavors you will pursue in your life?

Getting the most out of your education is analogous to going to the gym every day to get maximum results for your body. Many consistent and intense workouts will lead you to the final result—a healthier, more fit body. But instead of muscles, you're working on your brain and your future!

Now, how can you leverage the enormous amount of resources and opportunities available to you at your school? To learn how, you'll need to learn about all the various components of the educational system. Because only after you have looked at all these different components will you know how to use them to your advantage to accomplish your educational goals.

HAVE A
CLEAR PLAN

The Resources in the Educational System

The School Catalog

As a student, you must first be aware that much of the legwork of learning how to make the educational system work for you starts at home, before you ever set foot on the school campus — and even before the first day of class begins. Though the school catalog is often seen as only a reference guide to which classes are offered each year, be aware that it holds key information that will help you make informed and calculated decisions about your education every step of the way.

Simply by browsing the school catalog, you can find an enormous amount of information, including which courses are offered, which clubs/organizations are available, and where the tutoring center and guidance counselors are located. You can also find important administrative information that will help you to register for classes and help you to stay focused on essential graduation requirements. Financial aid and health-related information can also be found in the catalog, along with information about honors programs, faculty research projects, and interdisciplinary studies programs. It's amazing how much information you can find in the school catalog, yet how undervalued and underused it is by many students.

You have to be keenly aware that the catalog is a critical component of your educational success formula because it comprehensively and systematically will tell you exactly what resources and opportunities are available at your school. Become very familiar with the catalog, highlight it, underline key points you want to remember, and bookmark pages you frequently reference. It shouldn't just sit on a shelf or in your closet. It needs to serve as a dynamic and comprehensive guide that will give you a road map to all the valuable resources and opportunities that your school offers. Think of it as part of the overall blueprint for succeeding in school.

Academic Departments

After becoming familiar with the school catalog, get familiar with the different academic departments that interest you, so you can figure out what key resources they offer. From a general standpoint, academic departments serve to provide a comprehensive list of courses and help to oversee the administrative details of these courses. But they really do a lot more. They help run clubs/organizations that may be directly related to your interests, provide academic counseling and mentoring, and schedule seminars and workshops that can help you to hone your skills and even help you to network with key faculty members. You can also get career guidance and help obtaining letters of recommendation for scholarship/grant applications or to support admissions to future schools.

As you can see, the academic departments provide a wealth of information and services that will help you significantly, so it's crucial that you become very familiar with the departments that interest you and use them to your advantage—that's what they're there for. Get as much information as you can, because the more information you obtain from the departments that interest you, the more potential opportunities you'll create for success in your education.

The first place you can start looking for information is on the bulletin board or in information folders that most departmental offices have. These will provide you essential information pertaining to the courses offered, upcoming seminars and workshops, ongoing faculty research projects, and lectures that visiting scholars present. You can get additional information by talking to an administrative assistant or faculty member, or even by asking one of your fellow students. Don't be shy about asking, because you have to remember this is *your* future we are talking about. The majority of people whom you seek advice from will be more than happy to answer your questions. We can't overemphasize the importance of developing a proactive mindset when it comes to doing what's necessary to reach your educational goals.

The Classroom

Let's now turn to one of the main places you will spend your time—the classroom. As simple as the classroom environment may seem, just like the academic department, you've got to think of the bigger picture rather than focusing on the basics. Just as a typical student may view the academic department as a place that only helps with the administrative services of courses, you've got to *not* think of the classroom as simply a place where you go to hear an instructor lecture. You have to learn to be just as proactive in the classroom as in every other area of your education.

For starters, it's important that before you even step into a classroom, you do a little research on each course you will take.

Get information about the format of each course, including the course outline, structure, the number of quizzes and exams, what books are required, the amount and type of homework typically given, what course projects will be assigned, and whether extra credit is available. This may seem like a lot of information to get for each course, but you can get this information very quickly through a simple conversation with either a student who has taken the course before, an administrator in the department, or the course instructor. It's important to get these facts because they'll allow you to gauge the difficulty and the time commitment for each course. You can then plan your schedule accordingly so you don't cram a bunch of "heavy" courses into one school session. Taking a lot of time-consuming and challenging courses in one session only hinders your learning process and can lower your overall grade-point average.

By getting basic information about each course, you will also be more prepared, confident, and focused when you take the course. There'll be no surprises. You'll know the basic game plan going into each course, which will then make it easier to succeed.

You should also get basic background information about the instructor. It's important to know if the instructor has a good reputation and if he/she is reputed to be knowledgeable, competent, fair, and respectful. Knowledgeable and competent means that the instructor not only has a clear understanding of the subject matter, but also knows how to effectively convey that knowledge to the students. You also need to know if the instructor is fair, because not grading fairly may indicate an inability to teach the subject matter effectively, or that the instructor has a tendency to assign only mediocre grades (for who knows what reason, but it can happen). Lastly, you need to know if the instructor is respectful. Being stuck with a disrespectful or condescending instructor for an entire school session is not fun, and more importantly, may affect your ability to learn. The best environment to learn in is a proactive, healthy, and happy environment in which the instructor enjoys teaching and will do whatever it takes to help students learn.

The Classroom Environment

Once you find out the basic information about the courses you'll be taking, it's then important to make sure that you're an active participant in those courses. This means not shying away when the teacher asks questions in class. It also means going to the instructor's office hours to clarify questions. Going to office hours can make the difference between having an average or a superior understanding of the course material. Bringing your knowledge up to the next level may simply involve going to the instructor's office hours a few times throughout the course.

Besides helping to solidify your knowledge in difficult subject areas, going to office hours also tells the instructor that you're serious about learning. The instructor may not only make sure you grasp important concepts, but in the event of a borderline final grade, you may be bumped up to the higher grade.

Where you sit in the classroom is also important. Research shows that students who sit closer to the front of the classroom earn higher grades. By sitting close to the front of the classroom, you're more inclined to pay attention, take more notes, and learn, rather than having your mind wander.

Forming study groups and working with positive, goal-oriented fellow students can also be a factor in your success. It's important to choose students who demonstrate a drive to perform well in their courses. When it's time to pick students to work on a course project or form a study group, if you have a choice, don't pick students who often show up to class late, sit in the back of the room and goof around, or don't seem motivated to learn. To succeed in your education, associate with students who you know are serious about learning and who share a common dream of success in their educational pursuits.

Lastly, whom you surround yourself with certainly plays a role in your ability to succeed. If you surround yourself with lazy, unmotivated, and pessimistic students, you better believe that it will be a lot harder for you to be successful than if you surround yourself with eager, motivated, and ambitious students who have high expectations for their education.

Assigned Course Textbook

The textbook assigned to you is an important factor in your ability to succeed in each course. But sometimes a textbook may be hard for you to understand—the writing may seem unclear to you or the writing style may seem dry and boring. Or perhaps the illustrations don't help you understand the concepts. It's critical for you to understand that the assigned textbook doesn't have to be the main textbook you learn from. There's a misconception among students that the assigned textbook is the only reference available to them throughout the course. As a result, students may have difficulty understanding the subject matter simply because they can't understand the assigned textbook.

While it may be true that a certain subject is challenging for you, sometimes you may have difficulty understanding a certain subject simply because the author of the textbook has a writing style that's incompatible with your way of learning. We will repeat this simple concept because it's one of the reasons why students have trouble learning: the author of your assigned textbook may simply have a writing style that's not compatible with your way of learning. Everyone learns differently. If you're having difficulty learning from your assigned textbook, go to the library and get one or two other textbooks *on the same subject by different authors*, and you might find learning those difficult subjects is a little easier — maybe even a lot easier!

The bottom line is that sometimes the best way to study is to have several textbooks written by different authors so that you can see the same subject taught from different viewpoints. This assures you that your way of learning will be taken into account, because you will have multiple sources to reference.

The Library

A great support to your learning lies in seeking references at your school library. Whether in the form of books, magazines, newspapers, videos, or online information, it's vital to your learning that you familiarize yourself with the library. If you really want to take your learning to the next level and not be a mediocre student who just gets by, you must use the library's resources. There's a good reason why you'll find so many of the A students in the library, searching the shelves for books that will help them learn.

Just as the classroom and the administrative department proved to have more valuable resources available than you may have imagined, the library too is loaded with resources. The key is that you've got to have a little bit of patience to understand how the library works. We say this because students sometimes get discouraged by the enormous volume of books, magazines, and other resources available. Also, the ability to retrieve information that's pertinent to their coursework may seem confusing and tedious to some. However, your school library should have pamphlets, brochures, or live tutorial presentations by librarians, which will show you how to retrieve valuable information quickly and effectively. Library computers are another resource to help you find information. Also, you can get personalized, one-on-one help from a librarian if needed.

Whether you're doing research for a term paper, need supplemental information to help you understand difficult subject matter, or want information about a personal interest or to complement learning from a club/organization you belong to, it's crucial to understand that the library is part of your "arsenal" of resources available to help you learn. Remember: if you aren't using all the resources available to you, including the library, then you aren't learning to your full potential.

And don't think that you've only got your school library available to you. If you think your school library is lacking, go to another school library or a public library. Usually, the best place to get virtually unlimited information is at the university libraries. Traditionally, these are loaded with almost everything you can imagine. And with the advent of the Internet as a key resource for learning, thousands of online journals, books, and magazines are available.

Using the Library to Study

Don't think of the library as just a place to find information. Many students go to the library simply to get away from the many distractions at home so they can study more effectively. The library is invaluable for engaging in serious, non-distracting study time. To make the most out of your study time at the library, though, you should be comfortable. This means picking a place to study that meets your needs—next to a window, tucked away in a corner somewhere, or close to the drinking fountain, or maybe at a place with a large table and a very comfortable chair. Whatever study environment you choose, make sure you make it your little home, as the more comfortable you are, the more likely you are to study effectively.

Some students even bring their own reading light, pillow, or slippers to make their study environment more comfortable. The bottom line is that you've got to do whatever you need to do to make sure your learning environment is comfortable for you.

Learning-Assistance Program/Tutoring Center

Even though you have taken all the necessary steps to try to under-stand the subject matter in courses that you may find difficult, includ-ing going to the teacher's office hours, consulting with classmates, and referencing additional textbooks at the library, if you still feel you are not learning course material adequately, there are more options avail-able to you. These are the learning-assistance program and tutoring opportunities. Unfortunately, many students do not take advantage of these benefits that their school provides for them. As a result, their academic performance suffers.

Your school should have learning-assistance opportunities available to you, whether in the form of organized centers that have group tutorial programs for difficult subjects, or programs in which you can be personally assigned to a tutor for individual attention. These services should also be free to registered students. They're available to ensure that you get the best education possible. However, like all the services available at your school, no one is going to force you to use them. You're the only person who has to live with your actions or lack of actions on a day-to-day basis. Even if you feel you can learn the subject matter effectively on your own, it's important to be aware that these programs exist, so you'll know where to go for help in the event that you find learning a particular subject difficult.

These learning-assistance programs are available to help not only students who have difficulty learning certain subjects, but also to help students reinforce knowledge they already have. Sometimes the best way to solidify your knowledge of a subject is to hear someone other than your instructor explain it to you. Hearing various explanations of the material can be helpful, and can really accelerate your learning.

Once you feel your knowledge in a subject is solid, you can then become a tutor at these learning-assistance centers if you wish. There's no better way to master a subject than by teaching it to someone else. So if you have the time and patience to teach, consider taking part in the valuable and very rewarding experience of tutoring.

Administrative Offices

Have you ever wondered what goes on in the administrative buildings? Sure, registering for classes happens there, and the offices of the main administrators are there, but did you know that some key resources are also in these buildings?

Resources Available in The Administrative Offices

- Student Development Center
- Career Guidance Center
- Counseling/ Mentoring Center
- Financial Aid Office
- Registrar's Office
- Student Government Office
- Faculty Offices

You'll find everything from the career guidance center to the counseling/mentoring center to the financial aid office in your school's administrative building. Your school may even have a student development center and an international studies center dedicated to providing services that will enrich your learning experience. These are all services that, similar to the tutoring services, are not required as part of your educational experience, but they're invaluable resources that complement your learning in the classroom.

Avoid thinking that learning takes place only in the classroom. It's not smart to think this way, and it does nothing for your educational future. Though the core of your learning will occur in the classroom, a great deal of it will happen in places like the mentoring and career guidance center, learning-assistance programs, and the student development office where you will find information about organizations, school events, and campus enrichment activities. It's really to your benefit to tap into all the different resources your school provides for you, because it is only then that your learning will become much more dynamic, comprehensive, and rewarding.

Mentoring / Counseling Center

If you're having difficulty finding motivation, or if you just don't know how to channel your energy effectively, go to the mentoring/counseling center. No, we're not saying go to the counseling center to get your head examined. If you're not familiar with this center, it's where guidance counselors provide you with academic advice, including giving you valuable information about the many different educational opportunities available to you. If needed, they also provide psychological counseling services to help students deal with personal issues they may be experiencing.

Regarding academic services, mentors/counselors can give you valuable insight into any questions you have. They can also evaluate your past and present academic record, and help you devise a plan that will enable you to reach your educational goals. If you don't yet have defined educational goals, they can work closely with you to create ones that are keyed to your interests and passions.

The process of creating goals usually involves identifying your strengths and weaknesses along with your passions. The mentor/counselor will then try to provide you with a step-by-step plan of action that's consistent with your character, is in line with your strengths, and makes sense to you.

But don't be shy about seeking a mentor/counselor who feels right to you. Though all will have your best interests in mind, finding one you feel comfortable with can make all the difference in the world. Remember, this is your education we're talking about, and your future, so you've got to do what it takes to make sure you're comfortable every step of the way.

Career Resource Center

The career resource center is available to help you find careers that may be a good fit. If you're unsure of what career you want to pursue, the career resource center is a great place to get clarity in this area. You can take tests that help match your strengths, weaknesses, and interests with potential career options. These tests even take into account your personality and behavioral characteristics. If you haven't taken one of these tests, it's definitely worth your time. At the very least, you will find out how your unique characteristics and personality traits can be matched to potential careers.

Consider going to the career resource center to take a career-placement test or to browse through the information folders that are available. This time will be well spent as an investment in your future.

Unfortunately, many students do not take advantage of the career resource center simply because they're not aware that this resource exists or because they don't grasp its significance. Keep in mind that finding a career that interests you can greatly motivate you to excel in school. This is because you'll be much more excited about pursuing your profession, and as a result, this will encourage you to perform better in school. This is why students whose minds are set on certain professions tend to outperform students who have no clarity or focus on what career they want to pursue in life.

Student Development Center

Another resource available to you is the student development center. This is yet another resource that will complement your learning in the classroom. The student development center is an informational resource center that provides students with an abundance of services. Traditionally, the center serves to inform students of clubs and organizations, campus activities, transportation and housing services, and outreach programs, including presentations and workshops that may be directly related to a student's personal, academic, and occupational interests. In a nutshell, the student development center complements the learning experience in an effort to make your education more fulfilling, enjoyable, and rewarding.

It's to your advantage to spend some time browsing the information folders and asking the administrative staff at the student development center about what services they offer and how these services can help you with your educational goals. It's especially advantageous for you to get information about clubs and organizations that are related to your interests. These have the potential to greatly enhance your educational experience and are a great way for you to grow and develop as an individual.

The student development office, with the many services you'll find there, will be your ticket to a much more enjoyable and enriching educational experience.

Conclusion

As you can see, the educational system has an abundance of resources available to you with the sole purpose of giving you the best education possible. Becoming successful in your educational journey is really about leveraging these many different resources and knowing how to use them to reach your full educational potential. It's also knowing that succeeding takes a lot more than just your personal efforts—it's actually a team effort. Everyone, including instructors, academic administrators, and the support staff of the various resource centers, plays key roles in your ability to succeed in your journey. How successful you ultimately become is directly determined by how much you take advantage of all these resources and the people who are there to help you.

Your future, as always, lies with you and your ability to take control of your life and create your destiny. A successful future doesn't just happen by wandering aimlessly and letting circumstances, events, and life just happen to you. You have to be confident in your educational journey and strive to reach your full potential. Remember: Your ability to succeed starts and ends with you. You've just got to make it happen!

We've now shown you the major resources and opportunities available to you in the educational system and how you can leverage them to your advantage. This sets the groundwork for your success. But there's really a lot more to becoming a successful student than just knowing what resources and opportunities are available and knowing how to use them. In the next chapter, you'll see what it truly means to unlock your full educational potential!

ACTION STEPS

☐ What would you like to accomplish in your education? Do you want to take part in certain clubs, sports teams, or organizations? Do you want to become involved in community outreach programs? How about achieving a certain grade-point average? What three steps can you take now to help you accomplish your educational goals?

☐ Look through your school catalog to discover the vast array of resources and opportunities available to you. Also, visit those academic departments that interest you and learn about the different resources they offer. Write down five new things you found in your school catalog or at the academic departments that can help you become a more successful student.

☐ Which classes are you planning to take next? Spend some time researching these classes. Find out what will be expected of you in terms of reading assignments, term papers, homework assignments, and what the quizzes/tests are like. What is the instructor like? Knowing this information will help you be more successful.

☐ Take advantage of your instructor's office hours to learn more about confusing/unclear course material. Also remember, you can go to the library and get an additional book or two on the same subject, but written by a different author, to help you if you are having difficulty learning a subject.

☐ Take a trip to your school library and spend some time learning about all the valuable resources available. Ask a librarian for assistance, if needed.

☐ Do you take advantage of the learning-assistance/tutoring opportunities at your school? How about the mentoring/counseling center? Career resource center? Student development center? If not, realize that these are all valuable resources available to help you learn and succeed in school.

Chapter 3

MAKING THE EDUCATIONAL SYSTEM WORK FOR YOU

We've talked about why an education is so important, and about all the different components of the educational system, but none of this matters if you don't apply this information to make it work for your life. Simply put, information is useless unless it is applied to do something useful. What good is it to know a lot of information if that information is not being applied in some way to better your life? It's analogous to saying that you are only *intelligent* because you know a lot of information, but you aren't really *smart* until you apply the information that you know. So being intelligent and being smart are entirely different things. What this chapter is about is teaching you how to be smart as a student, because if you want to maximize the results in your educational journey, you have to know *how to think and act smart every step of the way*.

Making the educational system work for you is about applying your knowledge so that you can effectively get the most out of your education. To do this, you must realize there are **three key principles** to achieving success, and without any one of them, your chances for success will be greatly limited.

Three Key Principles for Educational Success

These principles are the foundation of becoming successful in your educational pursuits—and not coincidentally, they are the foundation of becoming successful in any endeavor you choose to pursue in life. And we're not talking about revolutionary and breakthrough principles. We're talking about straightforward and proven principles that are so simple, it's amazing that every student doesn't follow them. And now you are about to learn the core principles that successful students use on a daily basis.

Principle #1: Have a Clear Road Map

The first key principle to succeeding in your educational journey is to **have a clear road map**. That is, to become successful in your educational pursuits, you must have a full understanding of what you're getting into and where you want to go.

Simply put, if you don't know the basic facts about what you're doing, how can you succeed at it? Think of it as playing a simple game of tennis. To play successfully, you need to have a basic understanding of how the game is played. You must know how to serve the ball, how to hit the ball within the boundaries of the court, and how to develop a sound strategy for winning the game. It is only then that you can develop the skills necessary for winning.

The same logic is true for your education. Though your education is far from a game, you need to think of it as an important endeavor requiring a clear understanding of what is involved. You must know all the different resources available to you and how to use them to your advantage, but most importantly, you must know how to apply these resources to achieve your *specific educational goals.* To do this successfully, you first need a clear understanding of your present situation and where you envision yourself in the future, and then you need specifically defined goals that will get you there.

Unfortunately, for many students, "getting there" never happens. Many students don't understand the importance of *having a clear road map* and how setting well-defined goals will allow them to systematically accomplish their educational objectives. They don't understand that a road map will provide them with the information, resources, and overall game plan for succeeding in school. And without these key factors, students are just wandering around from one school year to the next—in many cases with the best intentions—but end up graduating with a diploma that represents only a fraction of their true educational potential.

The inability of many students to succeed in their education then comes down to:

- **A lack of information;**
- **The inability to seek out resources; and**
- **The lack of an overall game plan for accomplishing their goals.**

Not having a clear road map, then, is what ultimately leads to many students' undoing.

"Would you tell me, please, which way I ought to go from here?"
"That depends a good deal on where you want to get to," said the Cat.
"I don't much care where" said Alice.

"Then it doesn't matter which way you go," said the Cat.
"—so long as I get somewhere," Alice added as an explanation.
"Oh, you're sure to do that," said the Cat, "if you only walk long enough."
— Lewis Carroll

This simple conversation from Lewis Carroll's *Alice in Wonderland* sums up why many students don't reach their full educational potential: they don't have a clear understanding or road map of their educational journey. So if you expect to succeed, it's important that you have a clear road map that will guide you every step of the way.

Your Road Map is Based on Your Desires and Ambitions

Your educational road map is based on your unique desires and ambitions, so you need to set specific short-term and long-term goals that are in line with these motivations. You have to figure out what you like to do, what interests you, and then set goals based on those interests.

If, for instance, you like working with computers, set some short-term goals to take computer-related courses so you can hone your skills and talents in this area. Also, you can set a short-term goal of joining a club or organization related to computers, so you can learn new information and network with other students who have similar interests.

Long-term goals might include graduating from school with an emphasis in computer information and technology, and using this educational background as a steppingstone to the ideal job you've always dreamed of. Or you could set a long-term goal to complete a personal computer-programming project that's been on your mind.

If your interests lie in helping others and you desire a career in medicine, dentistry, or nursing, then you could set short-term goals of taking biology courses or CPR training—or you could volunteer at the local hospital.

Long-term goals could include being accepted into medical, dental or nursing school. Another long-term goal might be to coordinate a school health-awareness event to educate students on proper health and nutrition.

Set Realistic Goals

Your short-term and long-term goals should be realistic. For instance, setting a short-term goal of starting medical school next year is unrealistic if you haven't even begun taking the many prerequisite courses needed before you could be considered for admission to medical school. Or saying that you would like to start a computer club at your school within the next three years doesn't show sincere desire, motivation, or initiative. Why not set a goal to start the computer club within the next one to two months and then do something weekly to research how you can make the club a success?

Have Written Goals

Along with setting realistic goals, write down your goals and assign them specific deadlines. Research has shown that the biggest factor in determining whether a goal will be achieved is whether the goal is written down and given a specific time frame for completion.

If a goal is written, that goal has a greater probability of not only being met, but of being met within the indicated time frame. Therefore, writing both short- and long-term goals is an absolute must if you want to be serious and truly committed to fulfilling the goals you set for yourself.

Goals Need to Be Dynamic

Setting goals also needs to be a dynamic process. Though you may have set specific educational goals for this year, life is an ever-changing and dynamic process, and committing to rigid goals is not practical given the way life works. If necessary, don't hesitate to be flexible about modifying your goals. If, for example, your goal is to join a film club at your school by the end of the first school session, and then you find out that no film club exists, don't be afraid to create one. Part of being successful involves sometimes thinking unconventionally and being flexible and adaptable in coming up with alternative solutions when current ones don't readily exist.

Use Your School's Valuable Resources To Accomplish Your Goals

Setting specific written and dynamic goals is just half of the formula for achieving success. You've also got to know how to tap into your school's valuable resources and use them to accomplish your educational goals. Whether it's through the different academic departments, library, tutoring center, career resource center, or by getting involved in clubs and organizations, using your school's many resources is the foundation for making your educational goals become your reality. It's also at the foundation of building a functional and healthy road map that will ensure your success.

And remember, if you need extra guidance in setting goals, or are uncertain about your future, the mentoring/counseling center is an invaluable resource. Advice from someone who has more experience and wisdom than you have can give you new insight and a fresh perspective on all the educational and career possibilities available to you.

Your Road Map is Unique to Only You!

With your short- and long-term goals shaping your future, remember that the road map you're following day to day to accomplish your goals *is unique and personal to you alone.* Every student will have his/ her own unique road map, and what's right for another student may not be right for you. So trying to follow your friend's, brother's, or sister's educational road map is not a smart way to go about your life as a student. Your specific map and overall educational journey must reflect you as an individual. There are no two people alike in this world, and therefore there certainly should not be two identical educational road maps.

What If You're Not Clear About Your Road Map?

Many students don't know what they want to do with their lives as they begin their educational journey, or even while they are making it. In fact, even late into their education, students sometimes make last-minute changes in what they ultimately want to do with their lives.

This is all part of the sometimes experimental, transitional, and normal process of trying to find something that feels right, makes sense, and is in line with desired long-term ambitions.

It's perfectly normal to sometimes not have a clear understanding or be entirely focused as a student. The fact that other students may know with certainty early on what they're destined to do with their lives doesn't mean that you have to know early on. Each student is unique, and thus every student will have his/her own educational journey, which involves a growing understanding of specific goals at different times.

However, it's advantageous for you to try to develop and commit to specific goals as early as possible. Goals give you a reason for wanting to go to school, for having a purpose greater than just sitting in a classroom and taking exams each academic year. Goals help define who you are, what your present situation is, and where you eventually see yourself in the future. Without goals, you're really just wandering around from one year to the next passing time. Having clearly defined, written goals not only gives you a reason for getting out of bed each morning, because you have a purpose, but it allows you to be a much more determined, focused, grounded, and ambitious individual. So it really is important to strategize and figure out as early as you can what your interests and passions are. And once you've done this, you can develop specific short- and long-term goals based on these motivations.

However, if you're still having difficulty developing written goals, your plan of action will be a little different from those students who have a clear understanding of their goals and future plans. Rather than your road map being one of setting specific educational and career-related goals and using your school's resources to meet them, your road map will be more exploratory. In this case, it will be all the more important for you to use your school's resources to help you get clear about your goals and your life.

Resources to Help You Get Clear About Your Goals and Your Life

To help you get clarity on possible goals and lifelong pursuits, use the mentoring/counseling center, the student development office, and the career resource center. You can get advice from experienced mentors/counselors about all the opportunities available to you, and learn from the wealth of information you'll find there. The student development office will inform you about clubs and organizations or school activities that may interest you. And at the career resource center, you'll also have access to basic information, statistics, and job characteristics of the many different careers to choose among. You can also take personality/character tests that will help you become more familiar with careers that may suit you. Your game plan, then, is to go to these centers to learn all you can about yourself, determine what really interests you, and become familiar with your strengths and weaknesses.

You should also set goals that will keep you active and constantly engaged in doing all you can to learn more about yourself by using your school's many resources. Just because you may not initially know your game plan for life doesn't make setting goals unimportant. Setting goals is more important than ever for you and for any student who doesn't have a clear vision of what they want to do with their lives. Your goal can simply be to use your school's resources to explore any interests you have. Only after you've discovered and cultivated your interests can you start to develop a clear plan of action—**a road map**—that will guide you to success in your educational pursuits!

Principle #1: A Wrap-up

Okay, now that you know the first real secret to becoming a successful student—have a clear road map—it's time to make this principle work for you! But before you do, you need to know that there are two more principles that are just as important. Unless you apply all three principles as a whole, they won't be as effective. Only by applying each of these principles throughout every step of your educational journey will you be able to achieve enormous and sustained educational success.

So having a clear road map is the foundation for making the educational system work for you. Knowing where you are and where you want to go, and setting goals that are in line with your interests and passions is at the core of building a healthy and productive future. And knowing how to effectively leverage the enormous amount of available resources in the educational system is essential to accomplishing your goals. But having the right goals and right resources really doesn't matter if you don't have the right mindset—which brings us to our next principle.

Principle #2: Have the Right Mindset

Having the right mindset is such an essential component for success that, without it, it really doesn't matter what information or resources you have or what goals you set for yourself. If you haven't developed the right mindset, it will be difficult for you to succeed. This explains why some students who come from a background of abundant resources and opportunities do poorly in school, while others who come from very humble beginnings and have limited means perform exceedingly well in school. Having the right mindset opens up the possibilities for success, and then the opportunities for achievement become endless. This is because having resources and opportunities at your disposal only gives you *the potential for success*, but having the right mindset gives you the understanding, clarity, and focus to do what's necessary to become successful.

But what does it mean to have the right mindset? Let's find out. Keep in mind that you're about to learn what drives the successful student to achieve success, despite a sometimes severely disadvantaged background.

A Strong Work Ethic

The most important factor that enables a student to succeed in his/her education is *having a strong work ethic*. This is a tried, true and time-tested component that to be a successful student, you must have a strong work ethic. There are simply no shortcuts to educational success.

Successful students, as compared with average students, work much harder and with greater efficiency to achieve their educational goals. This means they work longer hours and work more efficiently during those hours than the average student does. So, simply put, if you want to create a mindset similar to that of a successful student, you must motivate yourself to work harder, and also, you must work more efficiently.

What does it mean to work efficiently? It simply means your work effort is spent in a concentrated and focused manner. An important way to ensure that you work efficiently is by limiting distractions.

These distractions could include personal phone calls, "surfing" the Internet, watching television, or socializing with friends while working on school-related tasks. The successful student knows that his/her working time needs to be well spent. Focusing on getting maximum results means avoiding time-wasting activities of the average or poor-performing student. Though it is important to have fun in life, you've got to know how to prioritize your time and how to focus your energy when it comes to important schoolwork.

Be Disciplined

Having a strong work ethic also means *being disciplined*. This means not procrastinating, but taking the initiative and completing school assignments in a timely manner. Remember: Procrastination is not only the "thief of time," but also the thief of your life! You've got to develop the habit of finishing assignments in a time-dependent way — this means not putting them off until the last possible minute. As school tasks are assigned, you should get into the habit of trying to complete them earlier rather than later. You would be amazed at how much time is wasted by simply looking at a task, picking it up, and doing a tiny fraction of it, only to keep coming back to it many times before it finally gets completed.

Tasks should be approached in a manner that allows you to finish them as soon as they are assigned. By working responsibly in this way, you will have more energy and enthusiasm to complete your school-related tasks than if you procrastinate until the last possible minute — only to rush through the assignment in a half-hearted effort to complete it.

Form Good Habits

Having a strong work ethic also means you must *form good habits*. Successful students form good habits and allow those habits to control their actions, which in turn allows them to control their lives. One key habit of successful students is getting up earlier in the day. By getting up earlier, the successful student is able to work on important school assignments with minimal distractions before the school day even begins.

Getting up earlier also allows you time to plan and organize the rest of the day. Part of this planning and organizing involves writing down what the objectives and goals are for the day — just a short list that takes less than a minute to create, but one that has immense practical and motivational power. You would be amazed by how powerful this "daily task list" is and how everything you put on the list gets done.

The average or poor-performing student, on the other hand, sleeps in until the last possible moment only to drag him/herself out of bed, into the shower, and then into the kitchen to devour a quick breakfast before running off frantically to school. Develop the habit of getting a jump-start on your day by getting up earlier and completing important school assignments, and creating a daily task list before the day begins. Developing these habits is at the core of cultivating the right mindset, which will enable you to become a successful student.

Be Proactive

You can have a strong work ethic, but without *having a proactive mentality* in everything you do as a student, your work output is not going to be at its maximum capacity. What does being proactive mean? In a nutshell, it means having the ability to take charge of your life, regardless of any limitations or setbacks, in order to create a positive outcome. It means not sitting back waiting for success to come to you, but actively doing what you can on a day-to-day basis to ensure success will happen in your life.

If it is to be, it is up to me.

— William Johnson

Success comes only by doing. And doing simply means taking an action-oriented approach to accomplishing every goal you set for yourself. To make success happen, you've got to go out there and make it happen! Don't depend on others to make you successful—you have to create your own success.

One of the key ways that students become successful in their educational pursuits is by *envisioning their desired goals as already accomplished;* that is, they visualize themselves in their future. Next, they look at the path they must take to get there. By envisioning with passion and clarity the life they seek for themselves, they will have a much greater chance of achieving what it is they desire. Many Olympic athletes, movie celebrities, and successful business people have used this simple technique to get from their initial humble beginnings to their present life of extraordinary success. In fact, the great majority of successful people will tell you that one of their core secrets is their ability to project themselves into a place where their goals have already been achieved.

To really make this principle work, though, you must think with absolute conviction, determination, and clarity of the exact place you envision yourself to be, and you must do it often. The more you project yourself into this place, the more excited and passionate you'll become, and thus, the more action you'll take to ensure you will get there.

Move Forward by Setting Goals

It's important that you do something every day that moves you toward your goals, and it's equally important that you maintain confidence, motivation, and conviction in your pursuit of accomplishing your everyday goals. Successful students do this by clearly envisioning their goals, and then, based on these visions, they write down exactly what they want to accomplish and the corresponding time frame. They then make detailed plans and work on those plans daily to accomplish their many goals. The key as we've already mentioned is to *write down your goals*. Part of being proactive is to be motivated and confident in accomplishing your goals. It also means thinking clearly about your goals and detailing how you will accomplish them, including writing them down on paper. This is one of the surest ways you will accomplish them.

Be Excellence-oriented

Always do your very best to accomplish your educational endeavors. Remember, the person who is going to be most affected by your efforts, whether they are impressive or lackluster, is *you*! You've got a limited time in the educational system to develop good habits, characteristics, and a solid work ethic. Doing this early in your life will not only make you successful in your educational pursuits, but will instill within you a success-oriented attitude that you'll carry with you for the rest of your life. So, it really is to your advantage to develop the right mindset, attitude, and work ethic as early as you can.

Be Solution-oriented

Being solution-oriented simply means focusing on solutions rather than problems. Inevitably, you will encounter problems such as a difficult subject, an instructor you can't relate to, or a term paper you find challenging. By concentrating on the solutions rather than the problems, you'll reach your goals much faster. Learn how to be a problem solver when you experience any dilemma — it's your surest way to a swift resolution and a successful outcome!

Always Continue to Grow

If you aren't growing mentally, emotionally, and intellectually, then you stagnate or regress — neither of which is any good. Always continue to think of expanding your possibilities and exploring any new ideas and opportunities that come your way. Being open-minded is essential if you want to continue to grow. It means that you're able to move out of your comfort zone and accept anything that will keep you growing. This means you've got to do those things that you've been thinking about at school, but maybe were not motivated enough or just too shy to do. Whether those things are to join a club or an organization, take part in a leadership activity or academic contest, or join that sports team, it's important you take the initiative and get involved. Whatever your interests are, develop a growth mentality and seek out opportunities to foster your natural interests and curiosity, because if you don't, you're limiting your educational potential and not taking full advantage of your abilities.

Have the Right Attitude

"The greatest discovery of my generation is that human beings
can alter their lives by altering their attitudes of mind."
— William James

This quote sums up why it's so important to *have the right attitude* in everything you do, including your education. You can work on your schoolwork from dawn until midnight, and you can be as proactive as possible, but if you don't believe you'll become a successful student, then you probably won't. The power of having the right attitude and believing with absolute conviction is critical to success; without it, it will be very difficult to succeed. This is the simple belief of "mind over matter." That is, whatever you think or fully believe will eventually become your reality. That is why it's so important for you to develop the right attitude in everything you do in pursuit of your educational goals.

With the right attitude, you'll continually maintain a mindset of positive self-expectancy. That is, if you expect to be successful in your many educational goals, you will seldom be disappointed. Expecting to be successful in everything you do will instill within you the passion and drive to do whatever it takes to accomplish your goals. And this means being flexible to the possibility that your goals may be achieved in ways you never expected.

If, for instance, your goal is to join student government as a council member, but you find out that all the council member positions are already taken, don't be discouraged. Serve as the student-affairs representative instead. Both positions can be equally rewarding, and both provide important functions in student government. Being flexible in your expectations allows you to be realistic about the way life works. And having the right attitude allows you to have realistic expectations about your goals, including the occasional unexpected outcome.

Having the right attitude also allows you to be confident, excited, and unwavering in your approach to accomplishing your many educational goals. The right attitude will make it much easier for you to be more successful in your education than if you choose *not* to have the right attitude. This is simply demonstrated by the "living magnet" concept: life is like a magnet—you'll inevitably attract the people and circumstances into your life that relate directly to your thoughts, emotions, and actions. What you think about all the time, and what gets you excited, will lead you to act in a manner consistent with those thoughts and emotions. This will draw to you the people, circumstances, opportunities, and resources you need to achieve your goals. This is a powerful but very simple philosophy of life that can really take you far … fast!

To maintain the right attitude, it's important to associate with students who also have the right attitude and determination to reach their goals. The people you surround yourself with on a day-to-day basis will significantly influence your thoughts and actions. Successful students develop habits that allow them to continually associate with other students who are positive and success-oriented. Unsuccessful students tend to associate with those students who don't have goals, don't care about their educational future, and don't have a positive outlook on life.

It's important to surround yourself with people who support you and your goals. They should respect you and see you as you are and who you can become in the future, not who you were in the past.

> *Treat a person as he is, and he will remain as he is.*
> *Treat him as he could be, and he will become what he should be.*
> — Jimmy Johnson

Associating with people who view you as you were in the past won't help you to grow into the person you want to become. This is why it's imperative to find people whom you enjoy and can learn from and who are supportive and respectful of your desire to reach your goals and become a successful student.

Be Fail-proof

Being fail-proof means never giving up your desire to be the most successful student you can possibly become, because it is only when you give up that you ultimately fail. You'll inevitably encounter setbacks and obstacles in your education, but you can only say you've failed if you let these momentary setbacks and obstacles prevent you from ultimately reaching your goals and succeeding. So as a student, you've got to decide to make a commitment to yourself to never quit in your pursuit to reach your goals, even when you experience what may seem to be insurmountable obstacles. You've got to keep picking yourself up and persisting until you succeed!

When you stop making excuses for things that may happen in your education, you open your mind to all the different possibilities for success.

There are a thousand excuses for failure, but never a good reason.
— Mark Twain

Thomas Edison, inventor of the light bulb, was a master of this philosophy. It is noted that it took him 10,000 attempts before he successfully invented the light bulb. However, when people asked him about his many failed attempts, his reply was that he had not failed, but had in fact successfully eliminated many ways that didn't work. Each attempt brought him that much closer to his ultimate goal, from which we all benefit today.

We are all called to succeed in life—it is our destiny. However, it's ultimately up to you, and only you, to choose to succeed. You're the only one who can choose the thoughts and actions that will allow you to keep pushing forward to achieve your goals, or to give up and ultimately succumb to failure. You are in control of your educational destiny. Choose now to become fail-proof and to accept that failure is not an option in your pursuit of making your educational dreams become a reality.

Live a Balanced Life

To lead a prosperous, fulfilling, and enjoyable life, you've got to be well balanced. Sure, you can concentrate all your energy and time on trying to achieve your educational goals, but you need to step back and look at the bigger picture. How do you expect to be successful if you aren't living your life in a healthy and well-adjusted way?

What does well-adjusted mean? Besides getting enough sleep, eating healthy foods, and exercising regularly, it means being balanced in your life.

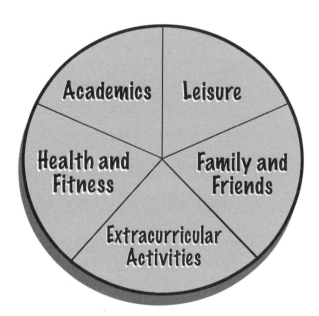

As a student, you've got to think of the bigger picture. This means not just studying all the time, but also getting involved in clubs and organizations, leadership activities, sports, and not forgetting to spend quality time with your family and friends. Remember: being balanced is important for not only your educational success, but also for your lifelong success.

Plan your life in a balanced way because when you're out of balance, you're not running your life at full capacity. For instance, if you neglect proper nutrition and exercise, then you won't have the energy you need to study efficiently. Similarly, if you spend all your time playing sports and don't take part in clubs and academic organizations, then you'll miss out on developing key relationships, learning new information, and cultivating important skills. And if you don't spend quality time with family and friends, then you may feel isolated and empty, which will surely affect your performance at school. The bottom line is that living a balanced life will allow you to live in a well-adjusted and healthy way. This in turn will give you the balanced life that you will need to be successful in both your educational and lifelong journey!

Now, you have been presented with **two key principles** to make your educational experience work for you. We've discussed our first key principle: *have a clear road map*. Then we moved on to our second key principle: *have the right mindset*. We discussed what each of these principles means and how each serves to create a successful student. But there is still one final principle to discuss—and in many ways it's the most important of the three. In fact without it, you're really just living your life daydreaming—we'll explain.

Principle #3: Take Action!

You can have a clear road map and the right mindset, but if you don't take action, you're really just engaging in an exercise of daydreaming. One of the most important factors that separate the successful student from the unsuccessful one is a clear and definite ability to take action.

If you look at society from a general standpoint, we all have dreams—and we're all on some sort of journey, in one way or another. Whether we're the individual who dreams of one day becoming a lawyer, the businessperson who dreams of one day becoming a CEO, or the homemaker who dreams of one day writing children's books, we've all got aspirations to do more. We all want to continue to evolve to a more accomplished and successful place. But for many people, the dream to evolve and continue to grow, unfortunately, remains only that—just a dream. Taking the next step to definitive action is an obstacle many people never overcome, accepting instead a life that is less than their full potential.

There is something truly powerful and exciting, but also intimidating and uncomfortable, about stepping out of your comfort zone and taking decisive action to accomplish your goals. A key factor in becoming successful is the ability to step into the unknown and take action—even though you may not know how you'll get to your final destination.

Take the first step in faith.
You don't have to see the whole staircase,
just take the first step.
— Dr. Martin Luther King Jr.

To be a successful student, then, you have to decide in advance that, no matter what, you'll take action! Even if you're unsure about precisely what action you should take, it's important to make a clear commitment to do something toward accomplishing your goals daily, without delaying for too long. Delaying is synonymous with procrastination, and both will get you nowhere.

The simple act of committing to doing something each day triggers a cascade of events that will result in new experiences and opportunities that can help you achieve your goals. And had you not taken any action, those new experiences and opportunities would not have become available to you.

It's also important that you not get caught up in the scenario of waiting for the "right time" or "right situation" to occur before you begin taking action toward accomplishing your goals. Theodore Roosevelt said, "Do what you can, with what you have, right where you are."

You've got to focus on the present moment and what you have right now—not on what you think your situation will be or what you think you may have in the future. Taking action based on hypothetical situations is not reliable nor is it the best use of your time. Visualize your dreams, think about what it will take for you to get there, and then take action—because living a life of dreaming without action is not living to your full potential!

The Wrap-up

We've discussed a lot in this chapter, but it's important that you fully understand the three key principles for achieving educational success:

- **Have a clear road map;**
- **Have the right mindset;**
- **Take action!**

We encourage you to go back and reread this chapter to get clarity on some of these principles, if needed. The information we've given you includes the *foundational success principles* that, if applied, have the ability to not only change your educational future, but change your life.

ACTION STEPS

❏ Your educational road map is based on your unique desires and ambitions in life. Set three short-term and long-term goals that are in line with these motivations. These can be both educational and lifelong goals. Write down these goals and give them specific timelines for accomplishing them. If needed, use the mentoring / counseling center, student development office, and career resource center to help you get clarity on developing your goals.

❏ Do you have the "right mindset" of a successful student? Do you have a strong work ethic? Are you disciplined? Do you have good study habits? What are five steps you can take that will make you a more successful student?

❏ Create a daily task list of items you need to complete each day before the day begins. This daily task list takes only a very short time to complete, but it has immense practical power to help you reach your goals!

❏ What type of attitude do you have in school? Whether you think you can or whether you think you can't do something, you are right. It is important to always believe in yourself and have an attitude that you will be able to achieve your dreams. What are three steps you can take to have a more successful attitude?

❏ Do you have a "fail-proof" attitude in life? Do you let momentary setbacks and obstacles defeat you, or do you quickly pick yourself up and move forward with a "never-give-up attitude" in achieving your goals? What are three steps you can take to have a fail-proof attitude?

❏ Are you living a balanced life? Do you get enough sleep, eat the right foods, exercise regularly, and have a balanced social life? What are three steps you can take to ensure that you live a more balanced life?

❏ The clear, distinguishing factor of what makes a person successful in his/her life is the ability to step into the unknown and take action. Are you taking daily action to reach your goals? If not, change your mindset, and take action!

PART II

We've set the groundwork for achieving educational success, but as you will see, there really is a lot more to becoming a successful student. Continue this journey with us into Part II of this book to discover that some of the most important information for achieving educational success is yet to come.

Chapter 4

GETTING A'S

Okay, it's on everyone's mind. Whether it's the science guru, the school football player, the ASB president, or the class socialite, students want to earn A grades in their coursework. So let's spend some time on this subject.

Let's dive right into why some students are consistently able to perform well academically while others are barely able to get by with C grades despite their best efforts. But more importantly, it is essential to understand exactly how successful students earn their A grades. What is it about their work ethic, habits, and character that leads these students to consistently achieve a high academic performance each school year?

Although these students are hard workers, you'll find that they have developed fundamental strategies and a plan-of-action approach toward their schoolwork that any poor- or average-performing student can take advantage of. And why not? Let's analyze how these students excel in their coursework, find out what their methods and strategies are, and distill them so that any student who has a sincere desire to earn high grades can, and will, given enough determination.

"I've found the formula for getting A's!"

Before we share with you the key strategies and techniques successful students use to earn their A grades, it's important for you to realize that you have the ability, the talent, and the potential to perform well academically—it's not beyond your reach. You have everything you need right now to accomplish this goal. Part of unlocking your full educational potential is believing in yourself—believing beyond a shadow of a doubt that you're capable of achieving any educational goal you set your mind to. You just need to realize this, passionately believe it, and then use your potential to earn those high grades you know you're fully capable of achieving and, more importantly, deserve!

Now let's move on to how you can succeed in school. What does it take to earn A grades? What exactly are the strategies and techniques A students use to perform well in school? Though a lot of hard work and commitment is involved, you may be surprised to learn that earning A grades fundamentally comes down to a systematic approach to learning schoolwork. It doesn't take a genius, a lot of money, the right school, or even a great family who'll support you every step of the way. In fact, earning A grades involves nothing more than learning some foundational principles. It comes down to only **three foundational principles** and their underlying components.

Principle #1: Develop the Proper Work Ethic

Put in the time, energy, and effort

The first major difference between A and C students is that A students do what is necessary to ensure that they won't be disappointed when they get their grades. They desire and expect to earn A's in their coursework, and they hold themselves to the A standard. More importantly, they understand that *to earn an A grade requires an investment of time, energy, and effort*—and this is what makes all the difference. They know that, like anything in life, success comes by working hard and by following through with those steps necessary to reach a desired outcome.

So what you must realize is that if you want to earn high grades in your coursework, there are simply no shortcuts to succeeding in school. You must put in the necessary time, energy, and effort to succeed. And because much of earning A grades comes down to studying, it's important that you are serious about the commitment it takes to learn course material effectively.

Study efficiently

You must also learn how to study efficiently. What do we mean? We mean that you can't just study for long periods of time and think you're using your study time in the most efficient way. When you study, there are strategies you need to implement to ensure that your study time is optimized for the best results. What are these strategies? Let's review them to show you how to maximize your study time to achieve your full learning potential.

Study in block increments

Realize that studying continuously for excessive amounts of time is counterproductive to learning. Research has shown that a typical student can only concentrate for about forty-five to fifty minutes at a time before learning becomes inefficient. If you want to maximize your learning, you have to break up your study time into forty-five to fifty-minute intervals with break periods between sessions. The breaks should be ten to fifteen minutes unless you're breaking for a meal.

During study breaks, try to reward yourself with something that you like to do. This can be watching TV, surfing the Internet, or calling a friend—anything you enjoy. But don't let your reward time turn into a two-hour phone call or an hour-long TV show. You have to keep yourself disciplined during the hours you've designated for studying. When your break passes the fifteen-minute point, stop whatever you're doing, and return to studying.

One of the key distinguishing factors between A and C students is that C students don't stay focused during their study hours. Instead, they let short breaks turn into long "play" breaks. They also become easily distracted by phone calls, the Internet, and other things during study hours. This impedes their ability to concentrate on schoolwork. It's important to reserve time for extended periods of fun activities, but this should definitely not be during your designated study hours.

Schedule your study time

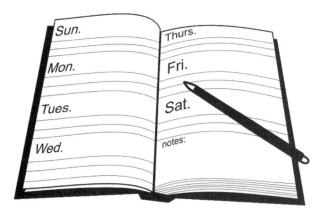

A good way to ensure that you concentrate and stay focused while studying is to schedule your study hours each day. By setting designated study hours and keeping yourself on a regular study regimen, you'll have more concentration and focus during study hours than if you study at random times. Also, the temptation to go hang out with your friends will be less appealing if you arrange study hours in advance. And just as setting daily goals is best accomplished by writing your goals down, you'll be more likely to follow through with your designated study hours if you write down those hours — preferably in a daily planner.

Find the right study environment

A key determinant of whether you will be effective and productive during your study hours is the environment you study in. This may seem simple, but many students tend to study in environments that are counterproductive to learning — in front of a TV set, in bed where it's too easy to fall asleep, around a boyfriend or girlfriend who craves attention, in a house where family members or friends are talking loudly and making distracting noises, or even at the beach or park, where there can be a lot of distractions going on. If you want to be serious about learning, you've got to *find an environment that will be conducive to learning*.

Some great study locations are the library, a designated study center at school, or an empty classroom. If you can control external factors such as the TV, Internet, phone, or pesky friends/family members, your room is also an excellent place to study. Just find an environment that works for you and then create a ritual of going to that place whenever you need to study. If you can, study at the same times each week at this location, as the continuity will be conducive to the learning process.

When you go to your designated study area, create the ideal study environment for yourself. Turn off your cell phone or TV, and bring some snacks and a water bottle. Make sure you have all the books and notes you'll need, and have paper and writing materials: pens, pencils and highlighters. Also, wear a watch or bring a clock so you'll know when to take breaks and when to get back to studying. Studying to classical music has also been shown to enhance the learning process because this type of music is conducive to concentrating.

The bottom line is, to earn those A grades, you've got to be serious about your study environment. How can you expect to study effectively if you are in an environment that is counterproductive to learning?

Pace yourself

If you want to truly understand subject matter, you have to study by pacing yourself over the duration of the course.

You can't expect to succeed at learning course material if you wait until the very last day to study for an exam. Sure, there are students who earn A grades studying this way, but the majority forget the material within days, if not hours, after the exam. You need to ask if you are doing yourself a favor by cramming until the last possible minute if you're just going to forget the information quickly. If you're one of those students who can study at the last minute and still earn A grades, this is a great accomplishment, but you have to remember that you're not fully maximizing your educational potential. Also, you aren't being responsible to your future if you study this way.

Fully grasping subject material requires studying in increments over the duration of the course. Research has shown that when you study something for a short while, set it down, and then come back to it later, *and do this repeatedly*, you'll learn the material at a far greater depth and proficiency than by last-minute cramming. Remember: Constant reinforcement is the mother of all learning. Though this may seem like common sense, you might be shocked to learn that many students study for only a day or two before an exam and never any more. If you fall into this category, it's important for you to break this habit now and start studying in a way that will benefit your future. Study by pacing yourself over the duration of the course instead of at the last possible minute. You need to study to learn, not just to get by—there's a big difference!

Okay, we've covered **principle #1: develop the proper work ethic**. You're a third of the way to learning the strategies of the A student. As you can see in our first principle, earning impressive grades is something that is attainable for any student who has enough drive, motivation, and guidance. Now let's move on to principle #2 where you will learn that you also need to **be smart in how you learn** to maximize your results!

Principle #2: Be Smart in How You Learn!

The second principle of the A student is to *be smart in how you learn*. What do we mean by this? A lot of things, but first, we want to let you know that developing a smart way of learning may require you to integrate new strategies into how you currently learn that may be different from what you are used to. It may take a little time and discipline to adopt these strategies into your study regimen, but it's important that you don't take too much time doing so, as these are some of the foundational strategies of the A student.

Being smart in how you learn involves taking advantage of the learning process in each of the three phases of learning: *before*, *during*, and *after class*. Let's review each of these learning phases to show you that earning high grades comes down to nothing more than a systematic approach to learning schoolwork.

Be smart in how you learn before class

Many students will not take action in school until their classes begin. Typical A students think differently. They know that to maximize their learning potential, they must become familiar with concepts that will be presented in class before the class even begins. To do this, they take two simple steps that give them a jump-start on their classes: 1) review the course syllabus; and 2) read the lecture assignments before each class session.

Course syllabus

The course syllabus serves as a navigational guide from which you can get valuable information. Therefore, read it as soon as it's given to you. It tells you everything from when exams are scheduled, to the books required, to what the weekly assignments will be, to how to contact the instructor if you have any questions or concerns. Also, it lets you know what's expected of you in terms of class participation and homework, and whether there will be any written and oral reports. The bottom line is, if you want to make sure you're adequately prepared for each course, and that no surprises occur that could compromise your ability to learn successfully, you need to refer to the syllabus throughout the course.

Pre-read

Besides becoming familiar with the course syllabus, many A students pre-read lecture assignments before they're presented in class. This means skimming reading assignments for general concepts and fundamental knowledge before coming to class. Just looking at the chapter headings and sub-topics and briefly skimming each page of your reading assignments will give you a general understanding of the subject matter and give you a huge advantage in learning class material. This pre-reading should take you no longer than ten to fifteen minutes.

Having a basic understanding of the subject matter before it's presented in class will allow you to more easily follow each lecture, take more effective notes during lectures, and study for less time afterward. This is because you will have developed a strong foundation of the material early on.

Now let's turn to learning in the classroom environment and how you can *be a smart student during class*.

Be Smart in How You Learn During Class

Okay, you've become familiar with the course syllabus and you've pre-read the lecture material—great! You're already well on your way to learning the course material in an effective and timely manner. Now, once you get to class, you need to implement strategies that will vastly increase your potential to learn during lectures. Let's examine these strategies.

Take excellent class notes

The first strategy to effective learning in class is to take excellent class notes. This means you must be *thorough* and *dynamic* in how you take notes. First, to be *thorough*, copy down anything your instructor writes on the board and says in class that you think is important. When in doubt, write it down—you can rewrite your notes later, but it's important that you get all the essential concepts presented. Teachers usually focus their lectures on what they feel is important—and what will be tested. So if you want to perform well, it's imperative to pay close attention to your lectures and take thorough notes.

Second, you've got to take *dynamic* notes. This means you should get into the habit of using shorthand and abbreviations. Also, if needed, use symbols, arrows, and boxes to show relationships between certain words or phrases. By taking notes this way, you'll be able to effectively write more information in less time, which will result in your taking more comprehensive notes.

To improve your note-taking ability, you can also use multicolored pens or pencils. Using different colors will enable you to distinguish between certain words or phrases, and it emphasizes the important points made in class. Also, it will help you more easily understand and interpret your notes when you review them later.

Sit in the front of the class to maximize learning

Where you sit in class is a key factor in learning. If you want to hear the instructor and see the board clearly, you need to *sit as close to the front of the room as possible*. This will help you take effective class notes and make sense of important lecture topics. Also, when sitting at the front of the class, you're less likely to be distracted, have your mind wander, and miss important points made by the instructor.

Be an active participant

To learn to your maximum potential, you need to be actively engaged in your classes. This means that instead of just passively taking notes, you need to participate in class discussions, ask questions, and take the initiative to be a strong contributor in both individual and team assignments. You can't just be a robotic learner who goes through the motions. You need to be fully engaged in the learning process. The classroom environment is a catalyst for a deeper understanding of course material, and this can be greatly enhanced by being an active participant in class.

Record lectures

For any lecture that's too fast-paced and information-packed for your note-taking ability, you always have the option of recording lectures. Simply bringing a recorder to those fast-paced lectures is the surest, and sometimes only way to get all the important points presented in class.

Also, by bringing a recorder to any lecture you feel is bogged down with detail, and even overwhelming to understand, you'll be able to relax and listen comfortably instead of trying to frantically take notes, hoping you'll get all the important concepts. Keep in mind that your recorder is yet another aid to help you with learning important information presented in class, and you should therefore use it whenever necessary.

We've shown you how to learn effectively in the classroom environment. Let's now turn to what you need to do after class to maximize your results!

Be Smart in How You Learn After Class

To be a smart student after class involves taking steps to ensure that you optimize your learning potential. This will keep you on the right track to earning those high grades. Let's review these steps.

Review class material immediately after class

It's important that, as soon as possible after each class, you review your notes and rewrite them into your own words. Information can be quickly forgotten after a lecture, so it's important to review your notes immediately and make sense out of them while the concepts are still fresh in your mind. Rewriting or typing your notes is an excellent way to learn course material. When you write or type information, you have a greater chance of understanding and remembering it. Rewriting your notes also is a great way to learn because rephrasing lecture material in your own words will make much more sense to you when you review your notes later.

Set goals for each study session

Before you dive into a study session, make a list of the goals you expect to accomplish for each session, and then check off each goal as you achieve it. By creating a checklist of your goals every time you study, you'll be much more likely to keep yourself honest and accountable for accomplishing them. Also setting study goals makes you much more likely to stay focused and committed to completing your objectives each time you study.

Get organized

Besides visualizing your ultimate goal, getting organized is another key strategy to earning A grades. A disorganized study area generally promotes a disorderly way of studying. You'll have a greater tendency to be unfocused and study ineffectively in a disordered environment. Simply organizing your study area promotes a more effective learning environment.

Study challenging and high-priority subjects first

Before you begin a study session, figure out which are the most challenging subjects and start by focusing on these. However, just as an athlete warms up with stretches and light exercises, you need to warm up your mind before you get to challenging material. If, for instance, you're studying math, start with a few easy problems that will engage your mind, make you mentally alert, and give you confidence before you move on to challenging material. Your mind is the freshest and most alert at the beginning of a study session, so you need to focus this time on the most challenging subjects. Also, figure out what assignments are urgent and most important and give those a high priority during each study session.

Make your study time engaging

Let's review specific ways to make your study time a more engaging process. You have your textbook reading assignment and your class notes in front of you. Now what? To be effective at studying reading assignments and class notes you have to "make them yours." What do we mean by this? We mean that you need to use strategies that will make you feel comfortable and engaged while you're learning course material.

First, *underline important words or phrases* when you read your textbook or notes. Also, you can use multicolored pens or pencils to emphasize key words or phrases you think are important so you can quickly review them later. Highlighters are also effective for emphasizing words or phrases. To make your notes more engaging, you can write key phrases or draw diagrams or pictures in the margins of your textbook pages or class notes. All these study strategies will help you to divide your reading assignments and class notes into more mean-ingful bits of information that will make sense to you and that you can more easily understand.

To make your study time even more engaging, try to *make your learn-ing experience fun*. Who says that studying has to be a boring and labor-intensive process? If done right, your study time can be exciting! When you study, create funny phrases, drawings, cartoons, or whatever will help you more effectively learn the subject matter. There's no wrong way to learn if the technique you use works for you. You can even cre-ate songs or rap to help you learn difficult concepts. It's important to use any of the above techniques that work for you to help you under-stand course material.

Another study strategy to make your learning experience more engaging is to *make flash cards*.

Write down definitions or phrases that are important for you to know, and make them into question/answer cards. Write a question on the front of the card and write the answer on the back. Take these cards everywhere you go, and when you have any free time—even a few minutes—take out your flash cards and start reviewing. Great places to review your flash cards include the grocery store, the doctor's office, a friend's house, while you're sitting in front of the TV, during a class break, or anywhere else where you might have some downtime.

Another technique to help you learn difficult concepts is to *use mnemonics*. These are simply words or phrases that help you to memorize information through word association. They're often used to help remember lists. For example, a simple mnemonic to remember the Great Lakes—Huron, Ontario, Michigan, Erie, and Superior—is HOMES. Each letter is the first letter of each of the lakes. Mnemonics can get a lot more complicated than this, but the bottom line is, become familiar with this learning strategy because it will make learning information, especially random facts, much easier to remember.

With all these ways to make your study time more engaging, learning should become a lot more straightforward and fun. If, however, you still have difficulty learning a subject, perhaps because you have no interest in it, then you can resort to pretending you enjoy the subject. We're not kidding! By pretending the subject you dislike is the most enjoyable and fascinating subject you've ever encountered—and you do this with passion and enthusiasm—you'll increase the probability of not only learning the subject, but of even liking it—maybe a lot! Instead of asking questions and thinking thoughts that express your dislike for a subject, try to reprogram your mind to make the subject feel more interesting and fun. This technique works, but only if you use a lot of passion and imagination.

Develop a strong foundation

Okay, we've shown you many different strategies and techniques for earning A grades. But to make sure you learn course material effectively, it's important to develop a strong understanding of course content each week before you move on to the new information presented in future lectures. This may seem simple enough, but it's yet another reason why students fall behind in learning: they simply don't develop a good grasp of general and preliminary course material before they move on to learning more advanced topics.

If you don't understand a topic in a lecture, do all you can to make sure you understand this material before you learn any new information that will be presented. Go to the teacher's office hours, consult with a tutor or classmate, or read additional textbooks to help you understand any confusing subject areas. It's important to sort out confusing topics right away, because waiting will only amplify the problem and lead to more confusion when future topics are presented.

Constant reinforcement of concepts

To develop a strong foundation, A students use many or all of the strategies and techniques we've given you, and they use them repeatedly. *Constant reinforcement* is truly the hallmark reason why A students earn those high grades. We can't overemphasize the importance of the simple concept of *constant reinforcement of the subject matter*. This means you need to review the subject matter you've already learned, and you need to review it frequently to make sure it stays fresh in your mind.

This will help you get a stronger and more proficient understanding of it—a level of understanding that will allow you to master your courses and become a high-performing student.

Visualize your goal

Another technique that will help you be more committed to achieving your study goals is to visualize your ultimate goal. This is the simple concept of *beginning with the end in mind*. Envision yourself in the future as a physician, architect, lawyer, successful businessperson, or musician—something you admire and aspire one day to be. Even hang a picture of your dream job in your study area. Visualizing your ultimate goal will motivate you to be dedicated to your study goals each week. This is particularly helpful on days when you may feel unfocused or distracted. By envisioning the end result when you study, you will be much more motivated to get there.

Prepare effectively for quizzes and exams

When it comes to preparing for quizzes and exams, it's important to spend an adequate amount of time doing so. Inadequate preparation is one of the biggest factors in poor performance on tested material. To ensure that you've learned course content before any quiz or exam, give yourself enough time to review your notes, the information presented in the lecture, and the textbook content. This might take a few days or weeks depending on the quantity and difficulty of the information.

In addition, for any major exam, get enough sleep the night before, because sleep deprivation is a key factor in poor test performance. Also, review your notes on the morning of an exam. This will engage your memory and help you be more mentally prepared for the test material. It will also help you recall everything you've studied. Lastly, some instructors make previous quizzes or exams available in an effort to help students understand the content more proficiently. This is another great way to learn difficult subject matter and ensure that you become familiar with what will be tested.

The Different Ways of Learning

Now that we've discussed the strategies A students use to earn their grades, it's important to understand that there are different ways of learning. Every student learns in a different way, and what may be effective for one student may not be effective for another. The different learning styles are **reading, hearing,** and **movement (kinesthetics)**. Through experimentation, you can figure out how you learn best. Sometimes, learning effectively involves a combination of the three styles.

If you learn best by **reading,** then you need to concentrate on learning material by reading your notes and the assignments from the textbook. If you record any lecture, write or type those lectures and read your notes instead of listening to a recording.

If you learn best by **hearing,** do whatever you can to "hear" your notes and your textbook reading assignments. When you study your class notes, instead of just reading them, read them out loud. Do the same when you read your textbook assignments. Reading out loud will deepen your understanding of the course material. Another strategy to learn by hearing is to record your class lectures and record yourself reading your assignments. Then listen to your recordings as often as is necessary to understand the subject matter. You can even play your recordings while doing things like cooking, surfing the Internet, or lying in bed. If you are an audio learner, teaching the subject matter to another person is also a good way of learning course material. Simply by hearing yourself teach, and by the very act of teaching, you'll be much more likely to learn.

The third way of learning is through **movement,** or **kinesthetics.** This simply means that learning is most effective when some type of movement accompanies it. Moving your arm, tapping your foot, bending your torso, walking while reading, or any other type of movement in which your muscles are actively involved is what kinesthetics is all about. If this is you, then start moving when you study: tap your toe, sway your wrist, or pace back and forth in your room with your notes in your hand. If kinesthetics is your way of learning, you need to start moving when you study — it's as simple as that!

Succeed in your own unique way

Throughout your school years, you'll see students learn and do things in different ways. Every student will have his/her own style of learning and way of succeeding in school, and what may be right for one student may not be right for another. Therefore, you need to find what works for you and do what you need to do to succeed. How much time other students spend studying or how they prepare for an exam or learn course material should have no influence on how you learn and succeed in school. This is important for you to remember because it's yet another reason why many students don't perform well in school: they tend to look too much at what other students are doing and, as a result, lose focus of their own unique abilities, talents, and ways of learning. If you really want to unlock your full educational potential, you simply have to be unconcerned with what others are doing and be the best *you* that you can be.

Okay, we've covered a lot of ground so far. Let's recap before we present the final principle to earning A grades. The first principle is to **develop the proper work ethic**, and the second is to **be smart in how you learn** — two foundational principles that are each composed of many different strategies and techniques for becoming an effective student. The third principle for earning A grades is to **be a proactive student**. What does this mean? Let's find out!

Principle #3: Be Proactive!

Being a proactive student means making academic efforts that go beyond what most students do to perform well in school. Just think about what a typical student does on a day-to-day basis to perform well in schoolwork, and then think about what he/she doesn't do. The difference is a "critical margin of success."

Let's review what this critical margin of success is all about. This margin of success is simply the little extra effort that you need to invest in your schoolwork, because it's this added effort that makes the difference between earning A grades or not. Now let's review what you need to do if you want to be serious about taking your academic performance to the next level.

Seek additional resources to help you learn

Being proactive means you seek additional resources to supplement your courses, if needed. Sometimes you may have difficulty learning from an assigned course textbook or from a certain instructor's style of teaching. If this happens, you need to know that additional resources are always available to you.

Traditionally, students seek help at the library, on the Internet, and at the school bookstore. However, three very important resources that students tend to underuse are tutors, the instructor's office hours, and networking.

Seek assistance from a tutor

Seeking assistance from a tutor is a vital resource that you can use to ensure that you sufficiently grasp difficult subject matter. Sometimes this is all that's needed to help you understand. Many students don't take the extra step of being tutored when they experience difficulty in a subject, and as a result, their understanding of material suffers, and so do their grades. To bring your academic mindset to the A level, you must take advantage of tutoring services if you have difficulty learning a subject.

And remember that becoming a tutor is one of the best ways to learn course material. If you think you have a good understanding of a subject, become a tutor and watch your understanding of that subject really take off!

Attend your instructor's office hours

There are several important reasons why you need to be comfortable with attending your instructor's office hours. The first is to allow you to better understand the subject matter. During office hours, the instructor can help you understand concepts that weren't clear to you when they were presented in class. Sometimes, just hearing the information presented to you one-on-one is all the help you need. Also, by attending office hours, you might learn about topics that weren't discussed in class and that can provide a more comprehensive picture of what was discussed.

The second reason to attend office hours is because this shows the instructor that you're serious about learning and that you care about your future. Both can be determining factors in earning a higher grade in your course.

Third, when you attend office hours, instructors might emphasize points that will be tested, and may even give you the benefit of the doubt if you get borderline grades on your tests. The bottom line is, to give your academic performance that extra edge, you need to attend office hours.

Network at school

To take your academic performance to the next level, you need to network at school. This means that you find other highly motivated students who'll be available to share information, study, and exchange questions and answers. By doing this, what could take you hours to learn on your own might take you only a half or a third of the time. Also, networking gives you the opportunity to develop lifelong friendships.

One major advantage of networking is that it enables you to coordinate studying with one or more students. This can be an invaluable way for you to succeed in school. When you study with others, you can teach and test each other, share class notes, and even motivate each other. This makes learning course material easier and more efficient. It will also result in a deeper and more proficient level of understanding difficult concepts.

However, you need to find the right students to study with, students who share your desire to learn and do well in school. Also, find students who you feel will contribute a synergy to the learning process. Studying with students who socialize too much or contribute little to the group is counterproductive to effective learning. If this occurs, modify your study group or your academic performance will be compromised. But remember: a study group should only complement your overall efforts—a good portion of your studying should be done on your own.

Networking at school can also allow you to gain a better understanding of future courses you plan to take. Simply by talking to other students who've taken courses you plan to take, you'll better understand the basics of these courses: their structure, teachers' expectations, and the best overall strategy for success. All this information will give you an edge before your courses even begin.

Another reason networking is so important is that it gives you access to the previous exams that some instructors make available. Viewing old exams allows you to test your knowledge before your instructors test you. Released exams are one way that instructors help students learn, and reviewing previous exams gives you a serious advantage.

And don't forget to network with instructors, administrators, and anyone else at your school who can be a valuable resource in helping you achieve your educational goals. Networking is a key way to succeed in school—and in life. It's therefore to your advantage to start networking now.

Summary of the Three Foundational Principles for Earning A's

Wanting A grades is one thing—being motivated enough to do what's necessary to earn those A grades is another. What separates the A student from the C student, as you have now learned, is the ability to:

- **Develop the Proper Work Ethic**
- **Be Smart in How You Learn**
- **Be Proactive**

You now know the *three foundational principles* for earning A grades. Incorporating these principles into your academic regimen is your ticket to earning higher grades. However, we haven't discussed the significance of what an A grade really means. We've only shown you the mechanics of how to earn A grades. It defeats the purpose of this chapter if we don't convey to you why taking your grades seriously is so important for both your educational and lifelong future. Why is it so important to earn A grades? What does earning an A grade really mean? Let's find out.

What Earning An "A" Grade Really Means

One of the main reasons why earning A grades and being highly educated is so important is because this indicates that you're an intelligent person. You've got to realize the significance and enormous impact of what this means. By being intelligent, you'll have the ability to convert all of your knowledge into "applied information"—otherwise known as being smart—to create a *significantly* better future for yourself. What kind of future are we talking about? We're talking about a future in which you'll be much more informed, engaged in, and connected to the world you live in. This will enable you to have a much better understanding of the world and all its complexities—but more importantly, how to succeed in it.

Everything you do in life, from succeeding in your career, to buying a house or car, to understanding how banking and credit card institutions operate, to being able to write and speak effectively, to understanding how to better live with people of different cultures and backgrounds, to having a better grasp of world affairs, the stock market, government, leadership, technology, business, religion, and anything else that you can possibly imagine all comes from being educated. And the more seriously you take your education, the greater potential you'll have for success in both your academic and lifelong endeavors!

It is through being educated that you will have a new perspective of the world—a perspective that will bring with it greater promise, fulfillment, and potential for a better future. So taking your education seriously and earning those impressive grades will give you the power and freedom to move toward your life goals with a confidence, certainty, and readiness that you otherwise may not have if you didn't take your education seriously. But this is really just half of the story.

The Other Half of the Story

The ability to earn impressive grades and to become highly educated not only means that you will know a lot of information that you can use to create a powerful future for yourself, but it also means that you will have the ability to think more analytically, more creatively, and with greater depth, vision, and clarity. So simply by taking your education seriously and striving to earn those high grades, you'll more effectively understand and interpret information and use it in practical and valuable ways.

Furthermore, the mere fact that you're able to earn high grades means that you have the ability to work hard, to work diligently, that you're responsible and persistent, and that you possess a driven and unyielding ambition to reach your goals. And for all these reasons, everyone from teachers to employers to college admissions representatives and your parents will look upon you as a person who takes life seriously and who shows great promise and potential for accomplishing great things in life!

Though all these people will place a high value on your ability to succeed in school, you've got to remember that the fundamental reason for learning is that it opens your mind to the world and brings with it greater knowledge and enlightenment—and *a chance* in life for a much better future. Regarding the power of an education, Oprah Winfrey said, "Every student deserves a chance—that is what they deserve." And that's what taking your education seriously can do for you—it gives you a chance to reach your full potential in life. Through unlocking your educational potential, you will unlock your ability to move forward in life with the knowledge you need to achieve any goal you set your mind to!

ACTION STEPS

❏ Are you putting in the necessary time, energy, and effort to earn high grades? What three steps can you take to be a high-performing student?

❏ How do you study for your courses? Do you study efficiently? Are you studying in block increments, pacing yourself, and eliminating distractions when you study? Do you have a study schedule? What steps can you take to improve the way you study?

❏ What steps do you take to prepare for each of your class lectures before they begin? Do you review the course syllabus and pre-read lecture topics? Get into the habit of taking action before each of your class lectures.

❏ What steps do you take during your class lectures to ensure that you get the most out of them? What new strategies presented in this chapter can you use to help you learn more effectively during class?

❏ Do you review lecture material immediately after each class lecture while the concepts are still fresh in your mind? If not, start reviewing your notes immediately after each class lecture.

❏ Make a list of the goals you expect to accomplish for each study session, and then check them off one at a time when you complete them.

❏ Constant reinforcement is one of the hallmark reasons why A students earn those high grades. Do you reinforce learning by reviewing topics you have previously studied?

❏ How do you learn most effectively? By reading, hearing, or kinesthetics? Maybe it's a combination of the three. Figure out how you learn best and study in this manner.

❏ Seek additional resources to help you learn if needed. For example, use a tutor, or take advantage of the instructor's office hours.

Chapter 5

TAKE AN ACTIVE ROLE IN EXTRACURRICULAR ACTIVITIES

If you want to take your education to the next level and experience a whole new way of learning, you need to get involved in extracurricular activities. There's a lot more to becoming successful in life than just going to classes every day and earning impressive grades. Sure, you may learn a lot academically, but you'll fall short in developing many crucial life skills that can only be developed outside of the classroom environment. And more importantly, you won't be able to fully explore and cultivate your unique talents and skills.

School is about more than just following an academic curriculum to fulfill graduation requirements. It's also about seeing your school as an all-encompassing learning environment that has the potential to teach you much more than what you can learn inside the classroom. In fact, what you learn outside the classroom can be just as important, if not more important, than what you learn inside the classroom. This is because many important character-building skills that are learned outside the classroom are directly applicable to succeeding in life.

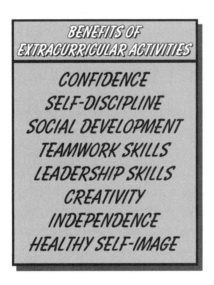

Leadership, teamwork, and social skills, along with learning how to become independent, creative, and hardworking, are all developed outside the classroom environment. Learning how to manage your time efficiently, becoming disciplined, and building self-confidence and a healthy self-image can also be learned outside the classroom. And it is through the many different extracurricular activities that your school makes available to you that these very important character traits can be learned and developed. Whether it's a club or organization, an athletic team, or the music or theater department, becoming involved in extracurricular activities is the key to taking your education to the next level!

Remember: Schools make extracurricular activities available because they want you to develop into a healthy and successful individual. They also want you to learn to your fullest potential, which means learning more than just textbook information, but also crucial character-building and life skills that will be your ticket to a successful future. If you just sit in the classroom, you can't possibly learn everything you need to know to become a healthy, well-rounded, and high-functioning individual with the ability to achieve your full potential. To get the most out of your education, you need to get involved in extracurricular activities — it's really that important!

What Does the Research Show?

To help you understand the significance of why getting involved in extracurricular activities is so incredibly important, let's look at what the research shows. According to research conducted by Darling, Caldwell, and Smith, it was found that students involved in extracurricular activities earn higher grades, develop better social skills, have higher aspirations in life, think more positively about academics, have a higher level of school commitment, and have a lower dropout rate. They also have a lower rate of drug use and of being arrested.

To support these findings, Mary Rombokas of Middle Tennessee State University found that students' intellectual and social development is enhanced when they participate in extracurricular activities. Those who did earned higher grades and developed valuable character and life skills that could be directly applied to succeeding in school and in lifelong endeavors. Also, it was found that extracurricular activities taught students to be more disciplined because of structured meetings, practice, or rehearsal schedules. And because students took part in activities including running, singing, acting, or organizing events, they gained a sense of responsibility and accomplishment when completing their activities.

As you can see, taking part in extracurricular activities is greatly beneficial. And the benefits just keep going!

Rombokas' study also found that analytical and creative problem-solving skills are improved when students take part in extracurricular activities. This was shown when students joined activities related to the arts. Students who performed music, acted in a play, or produced a work of art had to think more creatively, which improved both their creative and analytical skills.

But most of all, the research found, by joining extracurricular activities, students gained a greater sense of self-respect, self-esteem, and self-confidence. The sense of pride they experienced enhanced their self-image. And this made them want to work harder and do better in their extracurricular activities and in their coursework.

Another study, directed by Dr. Helen Ewald at Iowa State University, found that an improvement in organizational and time-management skills was correlated with students who took part in extracurricular activities. Because these activities took time away from academic coursework, students had to develop more efficient ways to complete both their academic assignments and the tasks in their extracurricular activities.

This same study found that extracurricular activities helped students stay in school. To join activities, students were required to meet minimum academic standards; and as a result, they were motivated to perform better in their academic coursework. Students would inevitably work harder at coursework because they wanted to make sure they met their school's academic requirements for being involved in school activities.

As you can see, taking part in extracurricular activities gives you a huge advantage both in performing well in school and in life. There's a wealth of benefits associated with involvement in school activities. It's up to you to take the first step and get involved now.

The Right Extracurricular Activity for You

You've learned that taking part in extracurricular activities is a crucial component to your educational experience and to your life goals. But which school activities are right for you? The simple answer is any activity you enjoy is right for you. Just think about which activities you feel will be fun and spend some time getting familiar with them. Your school may offer options that range from student government, to the baseball or soccer team, to the journalism or drama club, to the jazz band. You just need to think about what excites you and how you want to spend your free time — and then seek out those activities. But before you commit to any one activity, do some background research to make sure the activity you are interested in joining is right for you.

The first question you should ask yourself is, "Do I think I'll enjoy this activity?" Before you commit, make sure it really gets you excited. After all, it's your free time. Next, think about the overall purpose of the activity. Does it fit with your values and what you believe is an important use of your time? Then ask yourself what you can contribute to the activity and what you can gain. Next, ask yourself if the group of people associated with the activity interests you, and if you think you might establish good or even great relationships with them.

Another important factor to consider is how you feel your involvement in the activity can help you reach your academic and personal goals. How will it fit into your overall game plan? Will it help you accomplish your goals? One of the most important questions you should ask yourself is, "Can I balance my involvement in the school activity with my academic coursework?" Your first priority should be to perform well in your classes; only after you're able to ensure this should you consider extracurricular activities. Juggling too many undertakings at school will compromise your performance in both your schoolwork and the extracurricular activities you join. You need to find a good balance because only then will the benefits of taking part in extracurricular activities enhance your overall performance and motivation in school, both inside and outside the classroom.

Learn what Extracurricular Activities Your School Offers

It's important to explore what extracurricular activities your school makes available for you. The first place to look is in your school catalog, which has a wealth of information about what activities your school offers. Other sources include the school's Web site and academic departments. Each department should have a listing, in either a folder or on a bulletin board, of all the extracurricular activities it offers. Also, ask administrators or faculty members for information about extracurricular activities—they'll be able to assist you.

However, if you find out that your school doesn't offer a particular activity that interests you, don't worry, there are creative ways to deal with this.

Start Your Own Extracurricular Activity!

If your school doesn't have an extracurricular activity you enjoy, then just create one. Many students aren't aware that they have the power to create and run activities at school. In many instances, schools will help you by sponsoring it and possibly even funding the activity you want to create. Starting your own activity is one of the most exciting ventures to take part in. This is worth thinking about because doing it will be one of the most rewarding experiences of your educational years.

If you're really serious about creating an extracurricular activity, it's important to ask yourself why you want to start this activity in the first place. If it's because you think it will satisfy a previously unmet need at your school and can have a positive impact on students, then go for it! Creating something that adds value to the school is a win-win situation for everyone—for you, for the students, and for the school. You get the chance to organize, lead, and create a great learning experience, students get an opportunity to take part in the activity, and the school benefits because its students are more motivated to get involved. So starting an activity is a powerful undertaking that has the potential to impact a lot of people in a positive way.

Get a clear vision of what you want to create

Once you determine that you want to create an extracurricular activity at your school, it's important to get a clear vision of what you want to do. This can be anything from a school club, to a community service project, to an after-school sports team. School clubs typically include a science, history, or health club, a cooking, poetry, chess, language, or dance club, or just about any club you can imagine. If you're interested in starting a club, think about something that interests you, and then create a club based on that interest.

If your passion is to do something that involves the community, then create a community service project—arrange a blood drive, organize a recycling program, or teach children at a local elementary school. The list of possible ideas that can benefit the community can go on and on. Again, like starting a club, find something that interests you and that you're passionate about, and create a community service project based on this interest.

If, for instance, you're passionate about helping people who have a serious illness, you can create an event to help raise money for research and treatment. This could involve participants who run a marathon, with donations solicited for each lap completed around a track. This type of event is a great way to raise money to help those in need of medical care, and a great way to bond with fellow students and get to know people in the community.

If, however, your craving is to start an after-school sports team that doesn't yet exist at your school, then find students who are interested in your sport and check with your school about an acceptable location to play the games. The main idea is to find students who want to play and who'll be committed to practice sessions and game times.

Find a sponsor, enroll members, and start your new creation

Some activities may require a faculty moderator. If needed, find a faculty member who shares your interest and will help organize and oversee your activity. The sponsor is someone who'll play a mentoring role, attend many of the activity's meetings, and be available for guidance when questions arise. Once you've found your sponsor, you need to get students interested in joining your activity.

A great way is to post signs or hand out fliers at your school. You can also set up an information table where students can meet you, ask questions, and get further information. Once you've completed all the preliminary work to get students interested in joining, it's time to hold your first meeting.

At your first meeting, you need to be well organized and prepared to talk about your activity. You should have printed material to pass around that gives specific information, including what you'll be doing and when you'll be meeting. Also at this first meeting, you can get ideas and feedback from students about potential events or projects.

Next, it's important that you get leaders for your activity. Create as many positions as you feel are necessary for the health and productivity of your creation. When choosing positions, keep in mind that you need to hold elections in which all members can take part in electing their desired leaders.

Okay, we've covered the essentials of creating your own extracurricular activity. But whether you've decided to start your own activity or join an existing one, the bottom line is you need to get involved. You can't just be a passive student outside the classroom because this does nothing for your capabilities and talents. More importantly, it keeps you from reaching your full potential. To unlock your educational potential, you need to get motivated and get involved—it's that important!

Take an Active Role in Extracurricular Activities

If you're actively involved and committed you'll get a lot more from the time you spend in an extracurricular activity than if you're just a passive member. You'll learn a lot more, gain valuable teamwork and leadership experience, make great friends, and acquire valuable life skills that will allow you to become much more successful in accomplishing your academic and lifelong goals. So how can you get actively involved? Let's take a look.

One way to get more involved in an activity is to run for a leadership position such as president, vice president, secretary, or treasurer. Obviously, if you choose to run for president or vice president, your involvement and commitment will be a lot greater than if you choose to run for one of the less demanding positions. Just make sure you have enough time and will be able to make a full commitment if you decide to run for one of the more demanding positions. However, any position in an activity is important. It's just important that you get involved somehow so you can reap all the enormous benefits associated with becoming an active participant in an extracurricular activity.

Another way you can get involved is to spearhead an event hosted by your activity, or by volunteering to lead a committee in your organization. If, for instance, you join a health club, you can suggest that your organization host a blood drive and you can volunteer to help organize and lead the event. Or you can lead a committee that's responsible for getting speakers to present health-related topics. Another idea is to lead a committee that's in charge of organizing school-wide health events to benefit the students at your school, such as a health awareness day or a program that educates students about proper diet and nutrition.

Always keep in mind that you need to keep a proper balance between your coursework and your extracurricular activities. So, rather than joining many activities, try to focus on one or two in which you can put forth an honest effort and commitment. Trying to juggle too many activities can lead to a compromised performance in the activities and in your academic coursework. Also, you won't be able to fully appreciate and enjoy the activities if you're involved in too many of them.

Getting Involved in Extracurricular Activities Gives You an Edge

Taking part in extracurricular activities not only helps you develop in the areas of leadership, confidence, social skills, maturity, independence, and responsibility, it also gives you an edge in being accepted to a future school or hired for a competitive job. Joining activities shows that you have talents and capabilities outside of the academic environment and that you're dedicated to learning more than just course material. It also shows that you're able to juggle schoolwork and extracurricular activities simultaneously and that you're ambitious and motivated—not just a "bookworm" who only likes to study. Admissions committees realize the tremendous value of taking part in extracurricular activities, and therefore favor admitting students who've taken the initiative to participate in them.

Also, the more unique activities you can comfortably join, the more interesting you'll appear when applying for competitive schools and jobs. Anything that sets you apart from other students will give you an edge. If, for instance, you coordinate an outreach program that helps inner-city youth become motivated to make positive choices in their lives and stay in school, this will not only greatly help disadvantaged youths, but it will make you shine in the admissions process. Or if you create an Earth Awareness Day that helps make students aware of how to protect our planet, you may have an edge in the admissions process because you've done something exceptional.

Taking a leadership role in an extracurricular activity is another factor that can give you an edge in the admissions process. This is weighed heavily on your applications because it demonstrates responsibility, maturity, and dedication. Remember that taking on key roles in extracurricular activities such as president, vice president, or committee chair gives the impression that you aren't just an ordinary student, but a highly motivated and ambitious individual with great potential for success!

What's important is that you do something you feel passionate about—don't just join or start something, or pick a top position within an organization, to boost your admissions application. Trying to pad your application by taking part in activities or positions that you really aren't passionate about is a waste of your time and energy, and does nothing to tap into your true abilities. Do things that you enjoy and care about, because that's how you'll develop the core characteristics that will take you far in life.

Summer Breaks

During your academic years, you'll have summer breaks that may last several months. You've spent a whole school year working hard, and these breaks allow you to take time off from your normal school activities, relax, and enjoy the many summertime opportunities available to you. It's important, before your summer begins, that you think about how you want to spend your free time. Traditional activities during summer breaks are camps, athletics, study-abroad programs, academic workshops, work-study programs, and summer jobs. Though there's no right answer to what you ultimately decide to do during your summer breaks, there are definitely smart ways to spend your time off. Let's review.

The first question to ask yourself before your summer break begins is, "What can I do during my free time that's in line with my overall plans for my education and life goals?" If, for instance, you have an interest in the health sciences, then you can spend your summer breaks teaching CPR classes or working as a lifeguard. Or you can take a summer workshop to learn about human anatomy.

If you really like computers, you can work at a computer store to increase your knowledge of and proficiency with computers. Another idea is to get involved in a work-study program (if your school offers one) at the school computer lab. Work-study programs can usually be found through your school's financial aid department. If, however, you want to increase your knowledge of computers, you can take a summer course or two that will teach you more about computers.

If sports excite you, then join a summer team at your school or in the community. Your local community center should be able to provide you a complete listing of summer sports teams that are available.

Other good opportunities include a summer camp or taking part in a study-abroad program. Both will give you the opportunity to learn in a setting that is unique and different from what you may be accustomed to.

In a study-abroad program, you'll take one or more courses in another country. The idea of study-abroad programs is to learn in the classroom, but also to learn about a foreign country's way of life outside the classroom, including culture, history, traditions, music, customs, and more. Taking part in a study-abroad program is very exciting, and it's something you should consider seriously if you're comfortable spending a few months away from your family and friends.

Summer camps are another exciting way to spend your summer. There are *traditional summer camps* in which you spend a week or more up in the mountains learning about nature and taking part in outdoor activities such as hiking, swimming, and canoeing. There are also camps that include learning how to sing or dance, learning how to write or speak effectively, and learning how to work with computers. These are considered nontraditional camps because they're usually held at a school or other facility instead of in a camp-like environment. These nontraditional summer camps are very rewarding opportunities for you to learn and expand your mind. Rather than wasting your summer months playing video games or hanging out at the beach, you can take part in quality activities that are enjoyable and that will have a significant impact on your future.

The point of summer breaks is to enjoy yourself, so get involved in activities that excite you and that you feel will be rewarding. By taking part in these activities you'll grow as an individual and develop those characteristics that are crucial for success in both school and life.

When choosing summer activities, think about your short- and long-term goals and ask yourself whether joining a particular activity will foster your reaching these goals. Don't just pick random activities to join. Pull back and look at the overall picture of your life ambitions and make choices that are consistent with fulfilling them. Then, once you've decided how you want to spend your summer break, dive right in, get involved, and make the most of your summer!

The Wrap-up

John Wooden, the famous coach who led the UCLA basketball team to ten national championships, said that playing basketball is more than just a sport—it's more than just dribbling a ball down a court. Coach Wooden said that in basketball, you learn leadership, communication, teamwork, confidence, social skills, and integrity. Basketball provides the framework on which much more important life skills are developed.

By taking part in extracurricular activities, your ability to grow and develop is greatly enhanced. Extracurricular activities give you the tools, skills, and knowledge to be far more successful in life than if you only concentrated on the classroom environment. Realize that by taking part in activities you create a whole new way of learning that will be vital to your overall ability to succeed not only in your education, but also throughout your life.

And who knows, maybe your involvement in an extracurricular activity will turn into your lifelong career. Your membership in the school journalism club might turn into a career as a newspaper or magazine journalist. Your interest in speech and debate might turn into a career in law or politics. Your playing on the school baseball team might turn into a career in professional baseball. Who knows? But it is only through taking part in extracurricular activities that you will be able to take your educational potential to the next level. To truly maximize your educational potential, it's important to step outside the academic curriculum and get involved, because only by getting involved in extracurricular activities can you develop the characteristics, skills, and mindset to become much more successful!

ACTION STEPS

☐ Are you involved in extracurricular activities, or do you spend all of your time in the classroom? If not, what are one or two activities that you can get involved in that will help you become a more well-rounded student?

☐ Find out which extracurricular activities your school offers and explore those that interest you. Are these activities in line with your values and what you believe to be an important use of your time? What can you contribute to the activity and what do you feel you can gain? Understand that research clearly shows that there are numerous benefits to taking part in extracurricular activities.

☐ Is there any activity that you find really interesting, but your school is not offering? If so, research what you can do to create a new activity at your school.

☐ Realize that taking an active role in extracurricular activities is a key factor in becoming a successful student. What are two ways that you can get more involved in the extracurricular activities you join?

☐ What are you doing during your summer breaks? Find opportunities to help enrich your summer breaks. For example, look into summer camps, athletic activities, study-abroad programs, academic workshops, work-study programs, and employment opportunities.

Chapter 6

LEADERSHIP

Developing strong leadership skills is essential to becoming a successful student. You might think a leader is one who leads a team, governs the student body, or spearheads a school organization. But being a leader is something that can be characteristic of any student, in practically any endeavor. In the traditional sense, a leader is someone who guides and directs others. However, a much more important type of leader is one who can take charge of his/her life and do what's necessary to fulfill his/her true talents and ambitions.

We all want a life that's rewarding, prosperous, and successful, and that reflects our unique individuality. It is the individuals who set the goals, seek the opportunities, and create the lives they envision for themselves that are the true leaders in our society. Leaders are the people who are proactive in every aspect of their lives so they can reach their full potential.

It's no different in the educational system. Leader-like students are those who take charge of their educational future and do what is necessary to ensure their success both inside and outside of the classroom. They are proactive in every aspect of their educational journey, and as a result, their talents and full potential do not go to waste. They do what is necessary to develop themselves so that they can become as successful as possible. And that is what this chapter is about — teaching you how to be a leader within your own life so that you can develop the skills and abilities to succeed to your full potential in your educational journey.

Characteristics of a Great Leader

Let's now discuss more specifically what a leader is and how you can develop leader-like qualities so that you can reach your full educational potential!

A leader is proactive

Leaders take charge of their lives, set goals, and do what's necessary to accomplish them. They take the initiative, and are actively involved in becoming the best students they can be, both inside and outside the classroom. To do this, they understand that they must have a strong work ethic, be well organized, and have effective time-management skills.

> *Some people want it to happen, some wish*
> *it would happen, others make it happen.*
>
> —Michael Jordan

A leader is also decisive, and accomplishes goals by making effective decisions. Part of smart decision making is to make decisions in a timely way. Proactive leaders knows that pondering for too long or always "waiting for the right time" will compromise their ability to succeed.

> *If you put off everything till you're sure of it,*
> *you'll get nothing done.*
>
> — Norman Vincent Peale

Proactive leaders also remain open to change and to new ideas and different perspectives in accomplishing goals. They're willing to think creatively, which is particularly important when facing difficult obstacles to accomplish their dreams.

A leader is an optimist

A leader has a positive attitude and always looks for the best in others and in life. When they encounter setbacks, leaders learn from their experiences and become stronger, more resilient, and wiser. They don't worry about past disappointments, but are forward-thinking, continually moving themselves ahead to create new, positive, fulfilling experiences.

Part of being an optimist is being passionate about life and everything it has to offer. An optimistic leader cherishes life and is enthusiastic about each new day. This mindset helps leaders do their best, in school and in all of life's endeavors.

Leaders are also hopeful. They maintain realistic hope, meaning they're aware of all the challenges of their situation, but can also see the possibilities, opportunities, and the realization of their dreams. ·

He who does not hope to win has already lost.
— Jose Joaquin Olmedo

Lastly, an optimistic leader tries to make each new experience fun and exciting, both in school and in outside activities. This is particularly advantageous in stressful times. Leaders know that in order to live fully, they have to greet each new experience with enthusiasm.

A leader has strong interpersonal skills

Leaders are able to communicate effectively and relate well with others. They understand the importance and effectiveness of the different types of communication: *nonverbal, verbal,* and *written.* They strive to excel in these different areas because they know that communicating well is key to success and happiness in life.

A leader also listens to others and is not afraid to hear opposing views or to express opinions. Leaders look for diversity, rather than relying on the comfort of familiar thoughts and actions. They make sure they have all the information necessary to make the right decisions. And they make sure they aren't overly influenced by the last person they talk to or the loudest voice they hear. They make their decisions based on truth and facts.

A leader accepts responsibility for his/her life. Leaders never blame others for their own mistakes and failures. They also never criticize others publicly. They accept blame when appropriate, and try to make the changes needed for a successful outcome. They know that this sometimes means changing direction or focus or discontinuing an unhealthy relationship, even when this is painful.

A leader has strong values

Leaders maintain high standards and lead an ethical life. They are honest with themselves and others, and won't take shortcuts, especially at the expense of others. They say what they mean and follow through on what they say. They are straightforward, and they express their thoughts and feelings clearly, directly, and to the appropriate individuals.

A leader looks the part

Leaders know that how they look reflects on who they are. Appearance is the first impression one gives to others. Therefore, a leader knows that to make a good impression, to be taken seriously, and to instill confidence, one must look the part. How you look is directly related to how you will be treated—this is a reality of life, fair or not.

A leader has a never-give-up attitude

Leaders know that life is full of challenges, obstacles, and setbacks, and reaching goals requires never giving up in pursuit of them—no matter what the difficulties may be.

Become A Leader

Just learning the characteristics of a leader isn't enough to become one. You also need to strongly believe that you can lead your life in the direction you desire. Getting the results you want begins with having the right frame of mind. This means having confidence in yourself, a belief that you're able to take charge of your life, and that you have a "can do" attitude.

Creating the life you envision for yourself also means that you can't let circumstances and events dictate how your life unfolds. Rather, take charge of your life every step of the way and work at achieving your goals each day. This will allow you to become the person you aspire to be. Don't be like a leaf floating on a breeze, letting life take you wherever circumstances and events dictate. Take control of your destiny and create the life you know you're meant to have, and more importantly, deserve!

Regarding your education, don't be the student who just shows up to class and does only the bare minimum to get by. Learn to develop leadership characteristics so that you can become as successful as possible both inside and outside the classroom.

Become a Leader in the Classroom

Becoming a leader in the classroom means being proactive in every aspect of the classroom environment. This means doing your best to learn the material taught in class, being an active participant in lectures, and getting involved in group projects, class discussions, and presentations.

You need a "take charge" attitude in the classroom. This means you don't stand on the sidelines, but get involved, ask questions, and share your thoughts. Also, it means that you should prepare for courses before they begin.

Preparing for courses in advance will help you to be better prepared for any potential challenges that lie ahead. The best way to become familiar with a course is to research the instructors, become familiar with the course curriculum, and talk to students who have taken the course. Simply by spending a little time in advance researching a course, you will save a great deal of time later.

Also, being a leader-like student means being enthusiastic about your courses, even though you may not like some of them. Coming into class with a negative attitude only sets you up for failure. You may have to take some courses that you find uninteresting or that are taught by boring instructors, but it's important you realize that to be successful in your education, a positive attitude is essential. Here are some strategies you can use to make uninteresting classes more enjoyable:

Pretend the class is exciting. If, for example, you take an anthropology class (the science of the history of the human race), and you find the subject uninteresting, make it more exciting by imagining yourself living in ancient times and what it would have been like to live during that time. The more details you can imagine, the more exciting it will be to study the subjects you find uninteresting.

Ask better questions. Instead of asking questions such as "Why is this class boring," or "Why do I not like this class," ask better questions and you'll get better answers. For instance, ask questions such as "How can this class be enjoyable," or "What would make this subject matter more interesting?" By asking these types of questions, you focus your energy on how the class can be interesting, rather than why it's not.

Look at the bigger, long-term picture. If, for instance, you find mathematics boring, think of how equations and solving problems can eventually lead you to become a computer engineer, financial analyst, or rocket scientist—fields that use math in their day-to-day tasks.

Finally, it's important to realize that there's no such thing as a "perfect student." Every student will face difficulties and setbacks in his/ her educational journey. It's therefore important to do your best each day in the classroom, and realize that experiencing challenges is just part of the learning process. So when facing challenges, move forward with the confidence and the understanding that they're a natural part of your growth and development.

Become a Leader Outside the Classroom

Just as it's important to become a leader inside the classroom, it's equally important to become a leader outside the classroom. This means getting involved in the activities that you find interesting. Don't be afraid to take part in any activity that excites you or will help you develop as an individual. Get out of your comfort zone and stretch yourself. Any activity that will cultivate your interests, passions, and talents is an activity worth considering.

Becoming a leader outside the classroom doesn't mean that you have to become a team captain or ASB president. It simply means looking within yourself to explore your interests, passions, and talents, and then cultivating those attributes that make you the unique and special person you are. You don't have to get out there and try everything that arouses your curiosity — although it won't hurt. Start with the activities that you've always wanted to try, but maybe were too shy or nervous to do, and then jump in — even if you might not feel entirely ready to do so.

> *Jump in! Even if you don't know how to swim.*
>
> — Mark Burnett

Becoming a leader outside the classroom means that you remain faithful to your talents and passions. It means stepping out of your comfort zone and getting involved so you can grow and develop as an individual. Exploring new opportunities and interests isn't always the easiest thing to do, but you must realize that it is only through the exploration of new ideas and interests — whether that's joining the soccer team, the journalism club, or taking part in the school play — that you allow your unique talents and passions to grow and flourish.

If you want to develop leadership skills in order to lead a group of people, it's important to get involved in those school activities that foster this ability. By taking part in activities such as student government, speech and debate, and Model United Nations, or by taking leadership positions in clubs/organizations or on a sports team, you'll develop the qualities that enable you to lead others. Confidence, persuasiveness, assertiveness, charisma, strength, integrity, and patience are all fundamental leadership qualities that can be learned, or improved upon, by taking on leadership roles at your school. Therefore, if one of your aspirations is to lead others, join those activities that will promote this ambition.

Whether it's pursuing those interests that will help you cultivate your talents, or developing the skills that will help you lead others, it's important that you get out there, get involved, become a leader within your own life, and develop to your full potential as a student. Because only then will you develop the attributes that will help you to become much more successful in both your educational and lifelong journey!

It is not the critic who counts, not the man who points out how the strong man stumbled or where the doer of good deeds could have done better. The credit belongs to the man who is actually in the arena whose face is marred by dust and sweat and blood who strives valiantly, who errs and comes short again and again, who knows the great enthusiasm, the great devotions who spends himself in a worthy cause, who at the best knows in the end the triumph of high achievements and who at worst if he fails at least fails while daring greatly so that his place shall never be with those timid souls who know neither victory nor defeat.

— Theodore Roosevelt

ACTION STEPS

❏ What leadership qualities do you possess? For example, are you proactive, do you have strong values, and do you have a never-give-up attitude? List three leadership qualities you possess. List three leadership qualities you would like to develop.

❏ Are you creating the type of life you envision for yourself, or do you let circumstances and events dictate how your life will unfold? Take steps now that will move you in the direction of living the life you envision.

❏ Are you a leader inside the classroom, or do you stand on the sidelines and not get involved? Realize that a proactive mentality in the classroom is key to educational success. How can you become a stronger leader inside of the classroom?

❏ Are you a leader outside of the classroom environment? Look within yourself to explore your interests, passions, and talents, and then take action to cultivate them. This means stepping outside of your comfort zone sometimes and getting involved so that you can grow as an individual.

❏ Who is a leader that you look up to (past or present) that you can learn from? What makes this person special to you? What steps can you take to develop those leadership qualities you admire about this leader?

Chapter 7

COMMUNICATION

Developing strong communication skills is one of the core components for success in both school and life. Knowing how to express your thoughts, feelings, ideas, and emotions through effective oral, written, and nonverbal communication maximizes your ability to achieve your goals. Think of communication as the gateway to creating and cultivating valuable relationships, whether they're formed at school, in the workplace, at home, or in social settings. These relationships are part of the overall landscape of life, and they shape your destiny, directly impacting your ability to be successful in every facet of your life.

The way we communicate with others and with ourselves ultimately determines the quality of our lives.

— Anthony Robbins

Almost every experience we have depends on communication. Developing great friendships, maintaining a healthy self-image, succeeding in school and the professional world, resolving challenges and conflicts, and fulfilling our dreams and ambitions are all connected in some way to the art of communication. That's why it's so important to know how to communicate effectively, and that's why we devote an entire chapter to teaching you the principles and strategies of how to successfully communicate.

There are three main forms of communication: **nonverbal**, **verbal**, and **written**. Each is part of the formula for successful communication, and therefore, each serve as an integral component of what effective communication is all about.

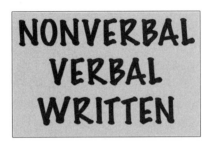

Nonverbal Communication

It's estimated that 60 to 90 percent of communication is conveyed without the use of spoken or written words — that is through *nonverbal communication*. What is "said" through the use of body language and other forms of nonverbal communication is just as important, if not more so, than what's spoken or written. For this reason, it's important to understand the different forms of nonverbal communication.

There are seven forms of nonverbal communication: **eye contact, facial expressions, gestures, posture and body orientation, proximity, paralinguistics, and humor.** Let's review how each of these plays a key role in the communication process.

> -Eye Contact
> -Facial Expressions
> -Gestures
> -Posture and
> Body Orientation
> -Proximity
> -Paralinguistics
> -Humor

Eye contact

Engaging others through eye contact is essential if you want to get your message across effectively. Not making eye contact when you speak to others may indicate insecurity, awkwardness, that you aren't being truthful, or that you feel others are insignificant. All of these negative attributes can reduce your ability to communicate effectively, regardless of the message you're trying to convey. Therefore, to ensure that your interpersonal communication isn't compromised, make eye contact with the people you speak with. This opens the flow of communication and conveys interest, concern, warmth, and credibility.

Don't make eye contact for too long, however, as this can be seen as hostile or threatening. A general rule is that eye contact should last for a few seconds at a time before breaking it. This allows the flow of communication to progress smoothly without the integrity of the message being lost.

Facial expressions

Facial expressions show others how you feel. It is important that your facial expressions are consistent with your message. The most universally recognized facial expression conveying friendliness, acceptance, happiness, and warmth is a simple smile. In many instances, a smile can help you accomplish more than what you say or write, so smile when you meet people and when you engage in conversation. You might be surprised by how effective a smile can be!

Other facial expressions that reveal your thoughts involve your eyes, forehead, brows, and lower face. The eyes easily project happiness, sadness, or surprise, while the forehead and brows express telltale signs of anger. The lower face can easily reveal when someone is happy, sad, or disappointed. The bottom line is that to convey the proper message to others, be conscious of your facial expressions because they play a key role in communication.

Gestures

How you gesture is also vital to communication. Common gestures include crossing your arms, nodding your head, pointing, or putting your hands on your hips. Each of these conveys a message to the people you talk to, whether you intend it or not. Therefore, it is important to be aware of what gestures you use when you speak.

Crossing your arms may convey that you disagree, are angry, or are symbolically closed to a conversation.

Open arms convey sincerity, honesty, and willingness to communicate. A simple nod of the head during a conversation conveys that you agree or that you understand what the other person is saying. Pointing, placing your hands on your hips, or clenching your fists are gestures to avoid in conversation, as they reflect negative attributes.

In general, be aware of the gestures you use because they carry a lot of weight in the communication process. They can sometimes even be the determining factor of whether someone is willing to continue conversing with you or not.

Posture and body orientation

How you posture and orient your body is important in communication. To be receptive, friendly, and approachable when you speak with others, stand straight up (but not militarily erect) with your shoulders back and lean slightly forward. This indicates that you're paying attention, that you're engaged in the conversation, and that you're interested in communicating. Slouching or not facing the person you're speaking with may show that you lack interest in the conversation, that you're bored or insecure, or that you don't place a high value on the other person. Excessive postural shifts, fidgeting, or tapping of the toes or fingers should also be avoided as they convey nervousness, irritability, or a feeling of discomfort. All of these examples of nonverbal communication should be avoided because they can cause a breakdown in the communication process.

Proximity

Your proximity to others during a conversation plays a role in communication. Cultural norms usually dictate the comfort level for each person, but it's generally accepted that when speaking to others, maintaining a distance of two to three feet is acceptable. If you get closer than this, others may feel that their "comfort zone" or "personal space" has been invaded. This can make them feel uneasy. A distance greater than two to three feet can make the conversation become impersonal and distant, and can lead others to feel uncomfortable. Therefore, when speaking to others, be aware of your proximity, as this can be a key factor in getting your message across.

Paralinguistics

Paralinguistics refers to the vocal elements that are characteristic of speaking. Using different vocal elements, it's possible for the same word to mean different things. We can tell if people are happy, angry, or nervous simply by how they speak, so it's important to be aware of the various vocal elements and how they factor into the communication process. The vocal elements are **tone, pitch, rhythm, timbre, loudness, and inflection.** Each can convey different meanings. For instance, speaking in a fast rhythm or with an erratic tone in your voice can convey to others that you're nervous or not focused in your thought process. Or speaking loudly with a high pitch in your voice can convey anger or surprise.

For maximum effectiveness, vary the vocal elements when speaking. This makes communication more engaging and dynamic. Not varying the vocal elements can result in a dull, monotonous delivery. So be cognizant of how you use your voice when communicating to others because how you speak plays an important role in the communication process.

Humor

Humor is the universal language of the world. When someone laughs, it decreases stress and makes people feel good. Humor is a great way to connect with others, so it's a great way to get your point across while letting people know that you're approachable, friendly, and charismatic. It's a good idea to try to incorporate humor into your everyday interactions, as this is one of the surest ways to make you enjoyable to be around. It's also one of the surest ways to become more successful in school and in life.

However, don't be too overzealous in using humor because you might not be taken seriously or might even offend someone. In general, humor is a great tool of nonverbal communication, so it's important that you're aware of this key element for successful communication.

The seven major areas of nonverbal communication are crucial to your ability to communicate effectively. It's important to understand how these nonverbal types of communication help convey your thoughts and feelings.

But nonverbal communication is only one form of communication. The next form is verbal communication, in which the spoken word is used rather than body language alone.

Verbal Communication

The ability to speak well in any situation, whether it's a casual one-on-one conversation or a presentation to a large group, is directly related to how successful you may ultimately become. It is a simple fact of life that the better you can verbally communicate with others, the easier your road to success.

In school, students with good communication skills are often the most successful. This is because a student who can clearly articulate his or her thoughts and feelings is the most likely to get better grades, excel in extracurricular activities, become a leader and even a role model to others. It's no different in the professional world. Those who have strong communication skills usually land the best jobs, are the first to be promoted, have the highest salaries, and generally out-compete those who don't.

Therefore, to ensure that your talents and abilities are not compromised because of poor communication skills, you must learn the fundamentals of effective verbal communication.

Fundamentals of Verbal Communication

There are many factors to be aware of in the verbal communication process; each plays an important role in your effectiveness at conveying your message to others. The first factor of successful verbal communication is the ability to *clearly communicate* your message.

Communicate your message clearly

A large part of verbal communication is how clearly you can communicate your message. The more clearly you are able to convey your message, the more successful you'll be. Below are guidelines to ensure that you get your message across in the most effective and understandable way.

Know the reason why you're communicating

Reasons to communicate can be to explain or teach, create understanding, build trust or mutual support, get input, or initiate an action. Knowing the specific reason for each communication will allow you to plan how you want to convey your message.

Organize your thoughts

Organize your thoughts into an overlying main point with sub-points. The more organized your thoughts, the clearer and more effective your verbal communication will be. Organization and clarity is power. Speaking without following a coherent thought process only compromises your message, and even your credibility.

Don't be complicated

The more elaborate our means of
communication, the less we communicate.

— Joseph Priestley

It's best to use well-known, everyday words instead of complicated, lengthy words when speaking. Also, try to use short sentences instead of long-winded, lengthy ones. Shorter, well-known words, as well as shorter, crisper sentences, carry more weight when speaking to others.

Think in terms of the other person

Think in terms of the other person before speaking to them. Before communicating your message, think about how your message may affect the other person and what his/her point of view may be.

Seek first to understand, then to be understood
— Steven R. Covey

Understanding where the other person is coming from will help you articulate your message more persuasively. It will also help the other person be more motivated and interested in hearing what you have to say.

Speak in positive terms

Always try to speak in positive terms. Bringing up negative topics, including speaking negatively about a person or situation, is the surest way to develop a negative reputation. No one enjoys being around negative people, so always try to speak positively when communicating with others. Express your positive messages clearly, directly, and often to the people you communicate with — your family, friends, fellow students, faculty members, or anyone you come in contact with throughout the day. Just as the body can't go for very long without nourishing food, relationships need to be nourished frequently to stay healthy and meaningful. Don't be afraid to tell others that you appreciate them, care about them, and are thankful for what they've done for you.

Praise and encouragement are too often in short supply. From the teenage years through adulthood, most people try to make their way through life with precious little encouragement. When we compliment, thank, and show interest in others, we lift them up and strengthen them. This is a powerful use of verbal communication.

On the other hand, when we criticize, nag, and insult, we rob others, along with ourselves, of confidence and energy. This can cause permanent damage and can even destroy relationships.

Listen effectively

The next element in successful communication is the ability to listen effectively.

When people talk, listen completely. Most people never listen.

— Ernest Hemingway

More than half of great communication is listening. Receiving accurate messages is critical to understanding others and developing healthy relationships. There are three components of good listening: **give your full attention**, **use your body language**, and **engage in responsive listening**.

Give your full attention

When listening, it's important that you *give the other person your full attention*. This means stop what you're doing, take the earphones out, turn away from the computer, and look directly into the eyes of the person speaking to you. Giving less than your full attention shows insincerity, disrespect, and unconcern for what the other person is saying to you.

Use your body language

The second component of good listening is to adjust your body language to indicate that you're attending to the person speaking. If you are seated, lean forward; if you're standing, turn toward the speaker. Don't be distracted by other people or activities, as this will compromise your ability to listen effectively.

Engage in responsive listening

The third component to good listening is to engage in responsive listening. This means you remember and respond to what you heard the person share with you. Avoid launching into your own story, feelings, and experiences. Immediately responding with advice, answers, and opinions can cut off communication, as it may imply that you aren't fully listening to what the other person is saying.

For example, if someone is sharing his/her career dreams and goals with you, don't make a mental list of your own while they're talking. Listen to and remember theirs. Also, listen and respond to the feelings they share—excitement, hope, anxiety, etc. Depending on what they've shared with you, you might say something like, "Being a lawyer sounds great. What got you interested in that career?" This is an open invitation to continue sharing.

When you engage in responsive listening, remember that it's important to listen to the whole message the other person wishes to share with you before you respond. This will allow you to respond appropriately and effectively.

Now that you know the components of effective listening, it's important to discuss why verbal communication sometimes breaks down. Knowing why will allow you to find solutions and make the communication process more successful.

Reasons Why the Verbal Communication Process Breaks Down

Killer remarks

We sometimes hear and may even be tempted to use "killer remarks." "You're stupid." "You're wasting your time, you'll never be good." "You're so immature." Killer remarks hurt, take away self-esteem and confidence, and can damage a relationship. We might think we're being funny when we say to an overweight person, "Did you get a varsity letter in eating?" This isn't funny, it's just mean-spirited.

One of the basic causes for all the trouble in the world today is that people talk too much and think too little. They act impulsively without thinking. I always try to think before I talk.

— Margaret Chase Smith

Sometimes killer remarks come in the guise of "just being honest" or "I am just telling you this for your own good." These aren't positive, helping words, but painful, negative remarks. Most of us can tell the difference between healthy criticism and the killer remark, which really is the other person venting at our expense.

If you have something difficult to say to someone, say it in the context of an expression of caring that contains no insults or personal attacks. It should also not be said when you're angry or frustrated. Focus on the specific issues or behaviors rather than on the individual. Your goal is to address the issue, solve the problem, make things better, and not hurt the other person.

Dishonesty

The verbal communication process can also break down because of dishonesty, which can destroy trust. If you've damaged a relationship by being dishonest, it's important to try to rebuild the bridge of communication with honesty, humility, and a sincere "I'm sorry."

WHAT DOES SHE THINK ABOUT ME?

Mind reading

We may think we know what others think or feel, but unless they tell us, we're guessing. When you're in doubt, or get mixed messages or no messages at all, simply ask the other person to clarify the issue. This will help keep communication lines intact and healthy rather than having them become compromised because of what you may think the other person is thinking.

If we're upset with people, we might use silence, ignore them, slam doors, and be uncooperative. We may expect others to be able to read our minds and know that we're upset, and know precisely why. Don't believe that others can read your mind by your behavior. If you have something to say, it's important to say it.

Using family members or friends as messengers

Using a family member or a friend as a go-between, spy, or keeper of secrets is another way that breakdowns in verbal communication occur. For example, complaining to your friend about something a mutual friend did to you doesn't solve the problem, but only creates a new one.

We may talk to third parties, perhaps a coworker or a friend, in hopes that the information will reach the person we have an issue with. Usually, the message gets back to the person inaccurately if at all. Again, if you have something to say, say it to the person yourself.

The other person may not want to communicate

If the person you're trying to communicate with doesn't respond, gives only one-word answers, or merely grunts, it probably means they wish to be left alone. Don't take it personally. People want to be left alone sometimes, for reasons that may have absolutely nothing to do with you. Everyone has a right to some "alone time." We all need space, freedom, and time to be alone. Not every thought or experience needs to be explored in conversation. Badgering others into discussion when they don't feel like talking is not a healthy way of communicating.

If, however, the person you're trying to communicate with is important to you, or if there's an important issue you need to discuss, ask if there's a time when the two of you can talk.

Inappropriate sarcasm

Too much sarcasm in a conversation can also cause a breakdown in the communication process. Sarcasm is an "end run" around the basic issue by using an indirect, slightly hurtful, or funny remark. This is different from being humorous about human nature and life's events. Too much sarcasm, especially in a serious discussion, creates an unhealthy imbalance, so be careful with sarcasm, and use it only if you feel it won't impair the verbal communication process.

Pitfall topics

Politics, religion, personal problems, and illnesses are among the conversation topics that may annoy and upset others. Also, trying to impose your personal beliefs and ideas on others isn't conducive to good communication. No one wants ideas and beliefs shoved in their face. Be confident about your convictions, but be aware that other people have their own. To keep verbal communication healthy and open, judge whether a topic is appropriate before bringing it up.

Also, avoid making sweeping statements and "sounding off" about sensitive topics, especially at the beginning of a conversation or relationship. A statement such as "I hate animals!", for example, could limit the number of people who are interested in getting to know you.

Strategies for Dealing with Communication Breakdowns

Now that we've discussed the many different ways that communication can break down, let's consider what to do if it happens.

Avoid knee-jerk responses

*Speak when you are angry and you'll
make the best speech you'll ever regret.*

— Dr. Laurence J. Peter

Sometimes, when we hear something we don't like, our immediate reaction is to fire back an angry outburst or hurtful remark. This is a knee-jerk response. Resist firing back when you're angry.

Try to find out more information that may be helpful in dealing with a hurtful remark. For example, you're told, "You are so selfish." The knee-jerk response might be, "No, you're the one who's selfish," or "You're crazy." A better response is "What do you mean?" We might then hear, "You spend all your time at work and with your friends. I feel like you don't care about me." Now you have information to work with and the beginnings of a dialogue that might move your communication to a better place.

Understand where the other person is coming from

It's always important to understand the other person's frame of mind when a breakdown in verbal communication occurs. There's usually an understandable explanation for his/her anger or frustration. Sometimes this may have nothing to do with you, but instead is because this individual is having problems at home or at work. Try to give others the benefit of the doubt.

When in doubt, check it out

Very few messages are perfectly clear; often there's ambiguity. If you're in any doubt about what was said, ask questions. "What do you mean?" "Can you explain?" Another strategy is to replay the message: "Do I understand that you're saying…?" The person can then say, "Right, you got it," or "That isn't what I meant to say," and explain more fully. Simply asking someone to explain a comment can usually clear up a misunderstanding.

Let it go

If someone says something hurtful to you, many times it's best to let it go. Don't waste any time thinking about or analyzing a remark, just ignore it. Remember: the only way a cruel remark can affect you is if you let it.

> *If someone offers you a gift and you decline*
> *to accept it, to whom does the gift belong?*
> — Buddha

You have the power to do as you wish with what you see and hear every day. Choose to not let negative remarks affect your ability to live your life to the fullest.

Keep your sense of humor

Sometimes, the best way to deal with an inappropriate remark or tense conversation is through laughter. Laughter can defuse criticism, keep a conversation from becoming uncomfortable or even hostile, and keep harmless missteps from becoming problems. Having a sense of humor about oneself is helpful as well. Inevitably, you'll encounter others who will make insensitive, inappropriate, or offensive comments. Usually, they do not mean to be hurtful, so try not to take it personally, and move on. If, however, this becomes a serious obstacle in a relationship, it then needs to be addressed.

Confront the critic

If someone continues to make hurtful or inappropriate remarks, you need to deal with this behavior. This can be direct: "What did you mean by that?" "Is there a problem we need to discuss?" Or you can be less direct and creative. For instance, when the individual says something hurtful, get up and leave the room. Most people will understand the quiet message you're conveying and will adjust their behavior accordingly.

Dealing with conflict can be difficult. Knowing when and how to address a conflictual issue can be a challenge. To lead to the successful outcome you want, address the situation tactfully and early on. It's important to resolve these issues with others before they grow bigger or even unmanageable.

Conflict can be a part of every healthy relationship

Conflict is part of the normal interaction between individuals, so you must accept it as part of life. Conflict is especially common in more intimate relationships such as between boyfriend and girlfriend, and among siblings and good friends. When we're close to others, we'll inevitably disagree, get in each other's way, step on toes, etc. This can happen over choosing what's for dinner, which TV programs to watch, and where and with whom to socialize. Almost everything we do can be a source of conflict. Among brothers and sisters we know it as sibling rivalry. But there's some contention in most relationships, since no one can have their way all the time. Flexibility, compromise, and sharing are crucial to resolving conflicts.

All healthy relationships have some sort of conflict. In resolving it, avoid accusations, labeling, generalizations, and unrelated issues. Also, do not bring up the past; confine the discussion to the present issue. Share your feelings rather than insults or put-downs. "I feel angry because … " is better than "You are …." By following these general guidelines, you'll resolve conflicts effectively and appropriately, rather than have them escalate unnecessarily.

How to Develop Your Communication Skills

There are many steps you can take to develop your verbal communication skills. Let's review them.

Communication Courses

At school you can enroll in communication courses in which you'll develop presentations to give to your class. Your presentations will be systematically critiqued, enabling you to develop strong verbal communication skills. As a result, you'll become more articulate, confident, organized, persuasive, engaging, compassionate, and dynamic. Over time, this invaluable experience will help you hone your speaking abilities both in day-to-day interactions and in large group settings.

Extracurricular Activities

You can also get involved in extracurricular activities that empha-size speaking skills: theater, student government, speech and debate, Model United Nations, or Mock Trial. These activities will help you to better organize your thoughts, develop presentations, cultivate per-suasive debating skills, and become more articulate. All of these are important for successful verbal communication.

Non-school Organizations

Another way to develop strong verbal communication skills is by get-ting involved in organizations outside of school. *Toastmasters Interna-tional* is an organization whose purpose is to help people strengthen their verbal communication skills. There are many local chapters. Par-ticipants meet regularly to give speeches that are critiqued for organi-zation, flow, style, vocalized pauses, and overall content. *Toastmasters International* has helped create some of the best speakers in the world, and it can help take your speaking ability to the next level.

Dale Carnegie is another organization that helps individuals develop their verbal communication skills. It offers a number of courses that teach in a supportive environment.

Books on Communication

You can also read books on communication to learn how to become a more effective communicator. There are numerous books available at your school, the retail store, and online that are written by experienced communicators who share their insights, techniques, and strategies for effective verbal communication.

Verbal Communication — A Wrap-up

Strong verbal communication is one of the surest ways to succeed in school and in your lifelong endeavors. To become proficient in your verbal communication—whether in day-to-day interactions or in group settings, you need to understand the techniques for developing powerful communication skills.

Take the necessary steps to develop your verbal communication skills now. Take classes, do extracurricular activities, join organizations, and read books on the subject. Also, speak as much as you can, because there's no better teacher than experience and just doing it!

Written Communication

We've discussed nonverbal and verbal communication. The ability to write effectively is equally important. Written communication is essential to communicating your ideas, feelings, and messages to others. What may be difficult or impossible to get across through verbal and nonverbal communication can be conveyed through writing.

Many students don't realize that the ability to write effectively can determine how successful they become, not only in school, but also in their social and career endeavors.

According to a study conducted by the National Governor's Association, writing is a threshold skill for both employment and promotion. In many instances, those who can't write well will not be hired or promoted. The study also found that effective written communication skills improve relationships and are a major determining factor in success in work-related projects. But it really goes a lot further than this.

We live in the technological and information age, and many of our everyday activities are directly related to writing. These include e-mail, instant messaging, blogs, discussion boards, and chat rooms, and, of course, letters and memos, the traditional forms of written communication. One can hardly get through a day without needing to communicate in some way to others through writing. And whether you want to believe it or not, your ability to write effectively plays a direct role in how others perceive you.

Do you misspell words, or use bad grammar or awkward sentence structure? How about writing without clearly articulating your message, or using run-on sentences? All of these give an impression of who you are, your thought process, and your ability to effectively convey information. Regardless of whether it's accurate or fair, your ability to write determines how people perceive what type of person you are, how intelligent you are, and how seriously you should be taken. All of these are determining factors in your ability to succeed in every aspect of your life—whether in school, your job, or socially related. This is why it's critical that you learn to write well.

While it's impossible to teach you how to write well in just one section of a chapter, there are fundamental principles and strategies of the successful writing process that are universal in any context or setting. We will show you what these principles and strategies are, and tell you what you can start doing right now to develop your writing skills.

Of course, when you write informally to friends and family members, you may use shorthand, jargon, slang, clichés, or abbreviated terms. This section is not intended to apply to informal writing. It applies to the more formal types of writing. These include writing papers, school- or business-related letters, sending e-mail correspondence to an instructor or colleague, and responding to a discussion board on a Web site.

Fundamentals of Effective Writing

State your point clearly

Writing is a transaction between the writer and reader, and it's the writer's responsibility to convey information in a clear and organized way. It's amazing how much is written sometimes, yet how unclear and ineffective a message can be. To write clearly, first gather your thoughts, organize them into coherent bits of information, and prioritize them in an order that makes sense.

Once you've organized your thoughts, then you can begin the writing process. The first sentence you write should clearly state the main point of your communication.

The following sentences should support that topic sentence: these may take the form of examples, reasons, evidence, and arguments to support your point.

When you move on to additional paragraphs, use transitional sentences so the reader can easily follow without becoming confused. Transitional sentences shift thoughts from one idea to the next while maintaining the cohesiveness of the message. A good transitional sentence shows the reader how two ideas connect, and at the same time it arouses the reader's curiosity about the new topic being introduced. To write a good transitional sentence:

Repeat a key word from the previous paragraph.

Refer to a fact or statement from the previous paragraph.

Use transitional words such as: *next, for example, besides, consequently, furthermore, likewise, meanwhile, also,* and *finally.*

Keep sentences and paragraphs short and simple

To write effectively, it's important that you try to *write shorter sentences rather than lengthy ones.* The longer the sentence, the more you may confuse the reader about the point you're trying to make. Some of this confusion may arise from introducing more than one idea per sentence. Each sentence should express no more than one idea. Also, avoid overly long paragraphs. When new ideas are introduced, make a new paragraph.

It is also better to *use plain and simple words* in most instances rather than long, complicated words. Don't make your readers have to resort to a dictionary to try to understand what you're writing. And don't try to impress your readers with a huge vocabulary at the expense of frustrating or confusing them. Readers just want the information they need in a form they can understand. Irrelevant or overly complicated information compromises your overall message.

To keep your writing simple and easy to read, avoid being redundant. If you've already expressed a point, it's unnecessary to bring it up again unless you're summarizing your main ideas at the end of a paragraph or at the close of your message. Redundancy only frustrates your readers and causes your overall message to become compromised. Redundancy also means using the same meaning twice in a phrase, such as: "the expectant pregnant woman" or "it's 2 p.m. in the afternoon." Add no unnecessary words to a sentence.

Use correct spelling and grammar

Misspelled words and bad grammar give the impression that you didn't spend much time in the writing process, that you might not care, and might not be very intelligent—all of which are obviously not good. Giving the reader these impressions undermines your credibility and weakens the point you're trying to make. Do everything you can to ensure proper spelling and grammar in your written communication.

Run a spelling and grammar check on your computer. You can also ask a friend or family member who's good at writing to proofread your work. It's also a good idea to own a dictionary, a thesaurus, and a grammar book.

In summary, correct spelling and grammar are essential if you want to ensure that your writing is taken seriously. Bad spelling and grammar will only compromise your ability to communicate effectively, and may even reflect negatively on your self-image. Therefore, always check your written communication for proper spelling and grammar.

Avoid slang, jargon, clichés, and misused words

It is important to not use slang, jargon, clichés, or misused words. Using any of these in written communication will only undermine the overall message.

Slang is invented or arbitrarily changed words that are part of an informal vocabulary. Examples of slang words are "cool" and "awesome." Slang words project a loose and informal style that should be avoided in formal writing. Using "say" instead of "tell me" at the beginning of a sentence is another example—"Say, how much does that cost?" is incorrect.

Jargon refers to language that is characteristic of a particular trade, profession, or group. An example is "All systems go," a term used by NASA. While this may be understood by some, it's best to use plain, simple words that everyone can understand. Jargon in written communication can confuse your reader and weaken your message.

Cliché means expressing a popular thought or idea that has been long overused and has lost its originality. Examples are, "bigger is better," "that takes the cake," and "think outside the box." Just as with slang and jargon, avoid using clichés, as they weaken the message.

Finally, don't misuse words in your writing, as they also weaken the message. For example, "I attended too meetings" is an incorrect use of the word "too"—it should be "two." Another example is "I don't care weather or not he goes." "Weather" is incorrect and should be replaced by "whether."

Use the active voice

Another important component of effective writing is to use the active voice. In English there are two different voices—the active and the passive. The active voice makes your sentences stronger, crisper, and more to the point. Also, it usually makes them shorter. An example of the active voice is "I increased my test score by studying." In comparison, the passive voice is "My test score was increased by the studying I did." Another example of the active voice is, "The teacher reviewed my project." The passive voice is, "My project was reviewed by the teacher." Sentences in the active voice flow more smoothly and have greater clarity and power. Always try to use the active voice in your writing.

Steps to Stronger Written Communication

Strong written communication requires that you continually engage in learning and writing. Effective writing doesn't happen overnight or come from reading one book on how to write well. It's an ongoing process of continually working to improve your writing skills.

Learning to write well is similar to learning to speak another language. The more you practice the better you become. You can't become fluent in a foreign language overnight. It requires constant practice, repetition, and effort *over time*. The same is true of learning to write well. The more you practice and learn, the more proficient a writer you'll become.

Let's review what you can do to improve your writing skills. First, you can take courses in English composition and writing. These courses will teach you the mechanics: you'll learn proper sentence structure, grammar, spelling, and how to write an effective paper. You'll also learn how to write with better direction, clarity, and focus.

Second, you can take any course that involves extensive reading—history, literature, or sociology, for example. There's a direct connection between reading and the ability to write well. Reading helps you understand the writing process better because the more you read, the more familiar you become with proper sentence structure, spelling, grammar, and word usage. Therefore, read as much as you can.

Keep in mind that not all reading has to come from your classes. Read anything that interests you: nonfiction books, magazines, newspapers, or Internet articles. If you enjoy mystery, romance, or science fiction, by all means read these. Reading actively engages your mind, and can be much more enjoyable and fulfilling than passively watching TV.

Keeping a journal is another way to improve your writing skills. Write about your experiences, what you learned from them, and how you feel the events of your day or week may have changed your life. A journal is a great way to express yourself and keep a record of your life. But it's the mechanics and the development of thoughts during the writing process that will help you improve your skills.

Written Communication — a Wrap-up

Writing is a key form of communication, so it's important to become as effective a writer as possible. Developing strong written communication skills only occurs over time by being actively engaged in the writing process. We've mentioned many different ways to help you develop your writing skills. The more ways you try, the more proficient you'll become at written communication.

And remember, written communication is connected to every facet of your life, including school, career, and social life. To ensure that your talents and ambitions aren't compromised by poor writing skills, do what's necessary to become effective at written communication.

ACTION STEPS

❏ Realize that there are three types of communication: *nonverbal, verbal,* and *written.* How well do you communicate in each of these areas? Where can you improve?

❏ Understand that there are seven major forms of nonverbal communication. Become aware of how you use these different types of communication in your everyday interactions with others.

❏ How clearly do you communicate your message when talking to others? Are you organized in your thought process? Do you think in terms of the other person when communicating? Are you a positive or negative communicator? What three steps can you take to improve your verbal communication skills?

❏ How well do you listen when you communicate with others? Do you talk more than you listen, or do you listen more than you talk? Use the three components of effective listening to learn how to become an effective listener: give your full attention, use your body language, and engage in responsive listening.

❏ Understand why the communication process can break down. Is too much sarcasm being used? What about pitfall topics or killer remarks? What steps can you take when the communication process breaks down?

❏ If someone has been making inappropriate and hurtful remarks to you, what steps can you take to effectively resolve the matter?

❏ What steps can you take to improve your verbal communication skills? Can you take a communication course, join an extracurricular activity that emphasizes communication (student government, theater, speech and debate), or read a book on communication?

❏ How are your written communication skills? Become familiar with the fundamental principles and strategies of effective writing. Realize that the ability to write effectively can determine how successful you may become, not only in school, but also in life!

Chapter 8

HEALTH AND FITNESS

This chapter is devoted to a subject that affects everything you do in life. It's about a subject so important to your everyday functioning that if you want to succeed in your educational journey, it's essential that you not only learn the principles in this chapter, but also that you apply them to your everyday life. We're talking about your health and creating and maintaining a body that will keep you energized and functioning at peak performance, so you'll have the stamina and drive to achieve your educational goals. How do you expect to become successful in your education if you run your body down with junk food and a daily regimen that doesn't include an exercise program that will give you the energy you'll need to accomplish your educational goals?

Having a healthy body is at the core of success not only in your education, but also in any endeavor you choose to pursue in life. Why do you think so many successful people make exercise and proper nutrition part of their everyday regimen? Successful people including CEOs of large companies, world leaders, entertainment moguls, doctors, lawyers and professional athletes know that in order to be at the top of their game, they have to keep their bodies in an optimally healthy state.

Think of your body as a car—a really expensive, quality car, like a Mercedes. Though this amazing car will look great and run for years, you have to maintain it by changing the oil and the air filter, replacing leaky hoses, replenishing water and coolant, and washing it to prevent dirt and rust from accumulating. Why wouldn't you take this same approach with your own body—the most complicated and high-tech machine on the planet?

Far too many students neglect their bodies and then wonder why they're always tired, why they don't have the stamina to get through the day, and why they lack the focus and motivation to set and meet the goals that will allow them to reach their full educational potential. With a fit and healthy body, you'll be more ready to do what is necessary to reach your goals.

Fortunately, getting your body energized and maintaining it in a healthy state is easily attainable. You just need the desire for optimal health and the knowledge of what to do. This is what this chapter is all about—teaching you how to get your body into peak optimal health! Through small daily changes, this chapter will teach you how to get great and lasting results that will turn your body into a fit, energized, and turbo-charged machine so you can achieve your educational goals.

Are you ready to get your body into peak optimal health? Are you ready to move forward toward your educational goals with a body that's energized, fit, and unstoppable? If so, then let's get started!

The Essentials of a Healthy Body

How do you get your body into peak optimal health? Fortunately, getting your body to an optimally healthy state is not some unsolvable mystery, nor is it an impossible task to achieve. In fact, getting your body to a healthy state involves only **four key principles**. These principles are at the core of producing significant, lasting, and life-changing results. But before we reveal these four principles, it's important for us to tell you that it's only the *combination* of these principles, and only when they are *actively applied to your everyday life*, that you'll be able to transform your body into the energized, turbo-charged machine that it's capable of becoming. If any one of these principles is missing, then that is enough to cause an imbalance in your health. Therefore, it's important for you to not only understand each one of these principles for optimal health, but also that you learn how to actively apply them to your everyday life.

What are these four principles for optimal health? They are: **1) eat the right foods; 2) exercise regularly; 3) get the right amount of sleep; 4) engage in only those activities that promote a positive and healthy lifestyle**. That's it—nothing more and nothing less!

Though these four principles may seem straightforward and trivial to you, it's important you realize that a great number of students do not fully understand these principles and the significant role that they play in creating a healthy body. Nor do many students understand how to actively incorporate these principles into their everyday lives. This chapter is dedicated to both—teaching you the essentials of creating a healthy body, and teaching you how to incorporate these **four principles for optimal health** into your life.

Now let's get started with understanding the first of the **four principles for optimal health—eat the right foods**.

Principle #1: Have a Healthy Diet

The first thing you need to know is that it's not difficult to have a healthy diet to create and maintain a healthy body. Nor is it difficult to understand what proper nutrition is all about. Like many students, you may feel confused by what a healthy diet means.

The concept of vitamins, minerals, nutrients, and proper food portions may seem overwhelming to you, and the notion of eating to create both peak body and mind performance may be something you're not familiar with. If this is you, you're not alone. One of the great epidemics in the school system is unhealthy eating. Too many students eat a diet consisting of cheeseburgers, hot dogs, pizza, and French fries without considering what these food choices are really doing to their bodies.

According to the US Surgeon General, the number of overweight adolescents has tripled over the past twenty years and is now at epidemic proportions. Furthermore, being overweight and obese are now considered serious health and economic issues that plague the young. And according to the Centers for Disease Control and Prevention, one in three children born in the US in the year 2000 will become diabetic unless diet and exercise patterns change. And when it comes to eating the right portions, the Food, Nutrition and Consumer Services/USDA reports that only 2 percent of school-age children meet the daily requirements of all five food groups, with almost 20 percent of their daily calories coming from fats, oils, and sweets.

Though these statistics may be shocking, it's important you realize that they are very real, and represent a silent epidemic that's sweeping the nation. The reality is that students are vulnerable to becoming one of these statistics if they don't take their eating habits seriously. Becoming informed about your eating habits is your ticket to taking charge of your life and, more importantly, keeping these problems out of your life. Now on to learning what a healthy diet is all about, beginning with what you need to drink to stay healthy.

Healthy Drinking

If you're wondering what you need to drink to keep your body healthy, the answer is simple—actually very simple. *Water* is the most important energy drink there is. Your body is made mostly of water, and as a result, water is responsible for many of your essential life functions, including helping to deliver vital nutrients, energy, and messages to the billions of cells throughout your body. Water is the power drink that fuels your brain and body, and it allows you to think, move, and process information. In fact, everything you do from the time you get up to the time you go to sleep is powered in some way by the water in your body. So by not giving your body the essential water it needs every day, you deprive it of the core ingredient it needs to run its many functions.

It's no surprise that so many students go through the day feeling tired and sluggish and have difficulty staying mentally alert and focused. They're literally dehydrating their bodies every day by not drinking the necessary quantities of water their bodies crave.

Another reason for the lack of energy and decreased mental focus many students experience is their poor habit of substituting high-sugar and caffeinated beverages, including soft drinks and coffee, for vital water requirements. What students may not know is that these high-sugar and caffeinated drinks may taste good, but they provide a false sense of energy by overloading the body with sugar and giving an energy boost that's temporary at best. And then, after that temporary energy boost is gone, students are off to consume even more "false energy drinks," and the vicious cycle repeats. It's a cycle that runs the student down and negatively impacts the overall health.

If you look at the research on high sugar drinks, it has been shown that there is a direct link between consuming too much sugar and weight gain. For every additional daily serving of soda consumed, the risk of becoming obese increases by about 50 percent. A Harvard University study also supported this correlation by finding that those who drink soft drinks regularly are more likely to become overweight than those who do not. And it doesn't stop there.

As a result of becoming overweight, the risk of developing diabetes increases. Research also found that a high-sugar diet is linked to a low consumption of nutritious foods including grains, vegetables, fruits, and dairy. Students are filling themselves up with high-sugar and caffeinated drinks, and as a result they aren't consuming an adequate amount of high-yield, nutritious foods. Can you see where all this is going? The bottom line is that by drinking beverages such as soft drinks and coffee, you're not giving your body the proper fuel it needs to run at optimal efficiency. You're also compromising your health and creating a body that's less able to provide you with the energy and staying power you need to reach your full educational potential.

By now, it should be apparent to you how incredibly important it is to drink the right type of beverage each day. What you drink is directly related to how your body performs. If you want a high-performance body, you need to drink high-performance beverages that will give you lots of energy. Though water is the ultimate energy drink, sports drinks such as *Gatorade* and *PowerAde* do offer advantages for the serious athlete. These drinks provide electrolytes and carbohydrates that give your body an extra boost during long and intense workouts.

Other drinks that are good for you include 100% fruit juices because they're filled with vitamins and minerals. However, they're also filled with sugar, so you should either limit your intake of these beverages or mix juice with equal parts of water if you drink them frequently.

Along with fruit juices, you can enjoy the benefits of water with a whole-food supplement by adding *greens* such as the one from Earth's Promise Greens (www.tastelife.enzy.com) to your water. These greens are filled with fruit and vegetable nutrients and contain a healthy dose of fiber. Adding greens to your water is a great way to add flavor to it and get the essential vitamins, minerals, and fiber that you need each day. If you haven't tried "green drinks" before, we highly recommend them, as they are packed with nutrients in one powerful, tasty drink.

Regardless of the healthy beverages you choose to consume every day, you must drink the minimum requirement of water as well. How much water should you drink each day? Most experts agree that six to eight glasses of water is what you need to drink to keep your body properly hydrated. If you exercise, you need to drink more water. It's a good idea to carry a water bottle with you throughout the day, drink from it about every thirty minutes, and refill it whenever necessary. You need to drink water throughout the day because your body is constantly losing water through breathing, perspiration, urination, and bowel movements. So replenishing lost water is important to prevent dehydration. Being dehydrated is definitely not good because it leaves you feeling tired and sluggish, and it contributes to a loss of energy. Carrying a water bottle is a great way to prevent dehydration because it helps ensure that you get your adequate daily water intake.

Okay, let's now move on to healthy food. What foods do you need to eat to keep your body healthy, energized, and full of life? There's a lot more to healthy eating than you might imagine. However, eating to create a turbo-charged body isn't a difficult goal to achieve, nor is it something that requires much extra time and effort to learn. You just have to learn some of the basics of what healthy eating is all about, and then apply what you've learned to each of your meals. It's actually quite simple, and more importantly, creating healthy eating habits is what will give you the energy and vitality to achieve your educational goals.

Now, if you're ready to learn about foods that will turbo-charge your body and that will, quite simply, change your life, please continue. In the next section, you will learn about the foods that are directly responsible for producing some of the most efficiently built and high-performance bodies on this planet!

Healthy Eating for Maximum Performance

Healthy eating involves many different factors, but the one key factor that all healthy foods have in common is that they all come directly from nature. Good, healthy foods are grown, produced, and sold to you without added chemicals and without being processed in manufacturing plants. If a food has to be chemically altered while being grown, is taken through a multi-step manufacturing process, or has been packaged to preserve it for the next decade, then that food is probably not the healthiest choice. In a nutshell, healthy foods are *whole* foods that come directly from nature, such as fruits, beans, nuts, grains, fish, eggs, and oatmeal.

Your body is 100 percent natural, so what it needs for energy is 100 percent natural foods—it's really as simple as that. If you're wondering what you need to eat to create a healthy body, think natural foods because foods that come straight from nature are the foods that are guaranteed to give your body energy that doesn't come at a compromising price.

Another way of looking at eating healthy foods is to think of your body as an automobile. Just as an automobile needs high-grade fuel to run at maximum performance and efficiency, you need high-grade foods to keep your body running in an optimally healthy state. By eating high-grade foods, you give your body the fuel and the combustion power it needs to work harder, longer, and with higher efficiency. In comparison, low-grade foods have unwanted chemicals and byproducts that compromise your body's overall performance. The ingredients in low-grade foods, including hydrogenated oils, preservatives, salts, and concentrated sugar, contribute to your body's engine becoming sluggish, tired, and worn down. This is because low-grade foods are mostly made up of empty calories that have limited value and offer no real energy. Because there is no real nutritional value in these foods, your body becomes starved for nutrients and can no longer perform at maximum efficiency. The bottom line is that if you want your body to perform like a well-tuned automobile, you have to feed it high-energy foods that are concentrated with nutrients and packed with energy! Just remember the golden rule of healthy eating: the more natural you go, the more nutrients and energizing ingredients you'll find in the foods you eat!

However, there's a lot more to healthy eating than just concentrating on natural foods. There are many resources available to you for advice about healthy eating. These include magazine articles, health-related books, and scientific research publications about healthy eating.

But the US Department of Agriculture (USDA) has compiled the most up-to-date information about healthy eating, has made it easy to understand, and has made it available 24 hours a day, 7 days a week! You can find this information at www.mypyramid.gov. It's presented in a **Food Guide Pyramid** format with a customized eating plan designed just for you. It's true — you can see your own customized eating plan at this Web site simply by inputting some basic personal information about yourself. Let's examine this Food Guide Pyramid, because it's the basis for wholesome eating. Everything you need to know about healthy eating is given to you at this comprehensive Web site.

The Food Guide Pyramid

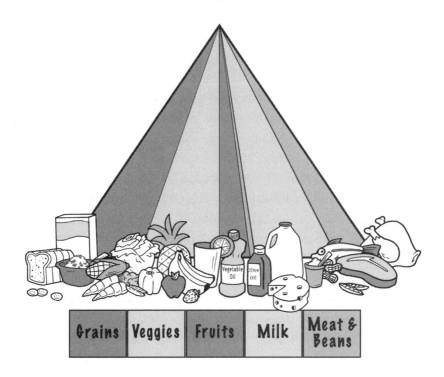

Grains | Veggies | Fruits | Milk | Meat & Beans

The Food Guide Pyramid is based on the most up-to-date information about healthy eating. It represents information compiled from scientific analysis and review from experts in the field of health and nutrition. Countless health and nutrition experts created the Food Guide Pyramid *so that you can have the best and most comprehensive information about what you need to eat to stay optimally healthy.* In a nutshell, the pyramid is a compilation of what you need to eat each day to make you a more healthy, energetic, and active individual. It's easy to understand, easy to use, and most importantly, easy to apply to your life *right now* so that you can get started on developing healthy eating habits immediately!

To start learning about the Food Guide Pyramid, go to www.mypyramid.gov. Here you'll find a pyramid that has five color bars representing the five basic food groups (grains, vegetables, fruits, milk, and meat and beans), and a sixth bar representing oils and discretionary food items (cookies, cakes, candy). Next, click on the *MyPyramid Menu Planner* tab. Then input your age, sex, weight, height, and estimated amount of daily physical activity, and hit the "submit" button. A comprehensive, customized eating plan will instantly appear that shows exactly what you need to eat each day to ensure that you're consuming a well-balanced diet — one that provides all the nutrients and energy you need to create and maintain a healthy body. Your eating plan will be based on the different food groups, and will give you tips about the most nutrient-packed foods and which foods to avoid.

If you click on any of the five food-group category names, an in-depth review of that food group is presented. If, for instance, you click on **MEAT AND BEANS**, a brief overview of how to make meat and beans part of a healthy meal is shown. You will find helpful information that is easy to understand, and more importantly, will help you easily incorporate healthy food choices into your daily meals immediately. It is to your advantage to use the information provided to get clarity about what food choices to choose when preparing meals.

You can also print a full report of your recommended daily food consumption from each of the five food groups. The report gives you a snapshot of what you need to eat each day to keep yourself on a healthy eating regimen. It's a great idea to hang the report on your wall so you're constantly reminded about proper nutrition and what you need to eat each day to get your body into peak optimal health.

Along with the Food Guide Pyramid report, you can print a Meal Tracking Worksheet that allows you to monitor your daily food intake and set goals for healthier eating. You can write your daily food items on the worksheet, organize them into their respective food groups, and calculate how much food (in ounces or cups) you consume.

Print a Meal Tracking Worksheet

This is a great way to get actively involved in your daily eating progress, and more importantly, it's a great way to understand the impact of what you put in your mouth before you do so. We highly recommend that you track your eating progress using the Meal Tracking Worksheet because closely analyzing how you eat each day is the only way to become familiar with your eating habits. It's also a great way for you to learn about proper nutrition. Use the Meal Tracking Worksheet until you become familiar with proper nutrition and confident that you're eating the right foods.

For an even more in-depth assessment, you can click on the **MY PYR-AMID TRACKER** tab at www.mypyramid.gov. This link will give you a detailed review of both your food consumption and physical activity. The major benefit of assessing these qualities together is that you'll be able to see how much energy you expend each day as a result of your physical activity, versus how much energy you take in as a result of your food consumption. This is important information because it allows you to monitor your energy input versus energy output. A thorough understanding of these energy levels will enable you to determine the right balance between how much food you need to eat each day and your physical activity level. Obviously, the more physically active you are, the more you need to eat to replace the energy you use.

Overall, the USDA Web site serves as the foundation for up-to-date and practical health and nutrition-related information and it is available to you 24 hours a day, 7 days a week *free of charge*. It's an invaluable resource for anyone who wants to better understand what foods are responsible for creating an optimally healthy body, and for anyone who wants expert advice on what good, wholesome nutrition is all about. But most importantly, this Web site provides a detailed and customized nutritional analysis, based on your distinctive personal information, to create a nutritional plan designed just for you so that you can get your body into peak optimal health.

Never before has it been so easy to take charge of your eating habits and to create a healthy lifestyle than it is today. It is now up to you to make a positive choice in your life and to decide to live each day in the healthiest way you can, starting with eating the right foods.

Dietary Guidelines

To make healthy eating even simpler, the USDA has created a Dietary Guidelines fact sheet that sums up healthy eating in a nutshell. So if you're confused about what food choices are healthy, just keep the following advice in mind because it comes straight from the USDA Dietary Guidelines found at www.mypyramid.gov/guidelines.

A healthy diet is one that:

- **Emphasizes fruits, vegetables, whole grains, and fat-free or low-fat milk and milk products;**
- **Includes lean meats, poultry, fish, beans, eggs, and nuts;**
- **Is low in saturated fats, trans fats, cholesterol, salt, and added sugars.**

If you stick to these three golden rules for healthy eating, you can't go wrong when choosing healthy foods for each meal. These golden rules are at the foundation of healthy eating, and they serve as the fundamental building blocks for what healthy eating is all about. Along with these three golden rules, it is also important that you know a few other key strategies for healthy eating.

Start Your Day with an Energizing Breakfast

Of all the meals of the day, breakfast is the most important. When you go to bed each night, you are essentially fasting the entire time you're asleep. Therefore, when you wake up in the morning, your body is starved and is craving nutrients and energy to become rejuvenated.

An energizing breakfast will help you jump-start your body and give it the fuel it needs to keep moving throughout the day. So don't neglect eating a solid, healthy breakfast because without it you'll feel sluggish and tired as the day progresses. And you won't be able to reach your full potential in trying to achieve your educational goals.

Fuel Your Body Throughout the Day

Along with eating the most important meal of the day—breakfast—you need to keep your body continuously energized by eating a healthy lunch and dinner. With busy schedules, students sometimes forgo eating a quality lunch or dinner, and instead graze on junk food or snacks to fill themselves up throughout the day. Remember that the three main meals of each day serve as the foundation to keeping your engine fueled and running at maximum efficiency. Without these three meals, your energy level will fall, you'll become lethargic, your mental alertness will decrease, and it will become difficult, if not impossible, to give your best each day. To prevent this, it's important that you schedule time to eat at least three full meals each day because these are the meals that will give you the energy you need to take charge of your day and to move forward with confidence, enthusiasm, and unstoppable energy!

Though three main meals is the norm, many nutrition experts agree that eating five or six "mini-meals" a day will give you greater energy and make your mind even more alert and focused. Fueling your body every couple of hours with small meals will continuously keep vital nutrients and energy flowing throughout your body all day long so you never hit energy lows.

Whether you choose to eat three full meals or five or six mini-meals each day, you need to figure out what eating regimen works best for your schedule and be consistent. Also, make sure the amount of food you eat each day is consistent with what the USDA recommends.

The Importance of Snacking

Along with eating regular meals, it's also important to snack throughout the day. Snacking keeps your energy levels up, and ensures that you don't hit energy lows, which will lead to mental and physical fatigue and a tendency to binge eat, especially on high-fat food items. With a constant supply of fuel, you'll be more alert, process information more efficiently, and excel in your overall performance throughout the day. The key is to eat small, energizing snacks between your regular meals. Nuts and raisins, a protein shake or smoothie, a cup of low-fat yogurt, fruit or cut veggies, or a granola bar are just some of the energizing snacks you can feed your body between meals to keep your energy levels maximized. Before you leave for the day, just remember to grab some snacks so you can munch on them whenever you feel hungry.

What Not to Eat

Okay, we've given you plenty of advice about what foods you should eat, but we haven't given you much advice about what foods to avoid. There are plenty of foods that contribute to clogged arteries, sluggishness, irritability, hyperactivity, and poor performance.

These foods are generally high in hydrogenated oils, salts, refined sugars, and LDL cholesterol, and as a result, they are foods that, in many instances, lack vital nutrients and energy.

These bad foods are energy draining because they take away your hunger and fill you up, but they don't give your body the vital nutrients and energy it needs. As a result, you become filled up on foods that may taste good and may give you temporary satisfaction, but in fact, these foods will lead you to feeling tired, sluggish, and even irritable.

This is because their side effects include increased blood pressure, increased blood-sugar levels, and even clogged arteries. This leads to compromised performance that will impact your ability to reach your true educational potential.

So what are these bad foods? Let's review.

The first major culprit in the bad food category is **processed foods**. These are foods that have been processed to increase the shelf life by adding hydrogenated fats, salts, and artificial preservatives, and by freezing, canning, irradiating, or pasteurizing. These are some of the different ways foods are processed. More specifically, you may be familiar with processed foods as anything from potato chips, crackers, and hot dogs, to canned soups, frozen meals, and white breads. They're found everywhere and usually taste very good, which is one of the reasons they're linked to so many health problems in America.

However, not all processed foods are bad for you. You just have to learn to read the nutrition labels on the packaged foods that appeal to you, to get an understanding of the type of food you're dealing with. If there's a high percentage of saturated fat, cholesterol, salt, or sugar, then this is a food item that you want to avoid entirely or eat sparingly.

The second major culprit in the bad food category is **fatty foods**. These include butter, margarine, cheeses, creams, and fatty meats. Everything from adding butter to toast, to adding cream cheese to a bagel, to eating oily chicken from a fast-food restaurant, is a food choice that should be eaten sparingly.

The last culprit in the bad food category is **sugary foods**. These include cake, candy, donuts, and cookies. These foods are high in sugar, and eating them leads to high blood-sugar levels, which leads to irritability, fatigue, and decreased performance. Staying away from high-sugar foods or eating them sparingly is the best way to ensure that you fuel your body with nutrition-rich foods that are filled with energy.

Practice the 90/10 Rule

The 90/10 rule is a rule based on human nature. We're built to enjoy life and everything it offers, so we can't possibly expect to follow an obsessively health-conscious diet every single day. There are so many different foods available, including rich chocolate cake, delicious pies, and tasty cookies, that it would be difficult, if not impossible, to have a diet that is void of these delicacies. The 90/10 rule simply states that you should eat healthy foods 90 percent of the time, while allowing yourself to eat whatever you want 10 percent of the time. If this means you want to enjoy a rich piece of chocolate cake or a milkshake, then so be it. The bottom line is that life wouldn't feel "natural" to you if you followed a strict health regimen without including at least a little bit of the many tasty treats life has to offer. So indulge a little, enjoy life, and have fun eating—but just remember, be responsible.

Okay, we've talked about the first principle for creating optimal health, **eat the right foods**. The second principle for creating optimal health is **exercise regularly**.

Principle #2: Exercise Regularly

Eating the right foods only gets you so far in attaining optimal health. Sure, you can eat extremely healthy every day and feel fine, but you still won't be able to achieve the level of health and well-being that a regular exercise program will give you. Hippocrates, the Greek physician known as the father of medicine, summed up the importance of exercise very simply when he stated, "Eating alone will not keep a man well; he must also take exercise." It's been known for centuries that exercise is one of the key principles to attaining an optimal state of well-being, and today it's stressed more than ever in the media, in the classroom, and through the many different exercise products that are continuously being introduced into the market.

The overwhelming benefits that come from a regular exercise program are indisputable. Scientific research continues to prove how exercise is directly linked to a healthier body—one that's stronger, more energetic, and much less susceptible to developing chronic diseases. The benefits of exercise are many; below are just some of the main reasons why exercising is such a crucial part of life.

A regular exercise program:

- **Strengthens bones and muscles, making them more able to take on life's challenges;**
- **Contributes to more energy and endurance;**
- **Helps prevent osteoporosis, cardiovascular disease, and non-insulin-dependent diabetes;**
- **Increases balance, coordination, and agility;**
- **Helps to control weight;**
- **Makes one feel and look better;**
- **Improves self-esteem, mood, and confidence.**

Exercise is truly the key to keeping your body energized, youthful, and full of life, and it allows you to attain a level of well-being that healthy eating alone can't give you. If you expect your body to deliver the energy you need to achieve even the most demanding goals, it's imperative that you get serious about taking part in a program of regular exercise.

What exactly is a good exercise program, and how much do you need to exercise? There's an abundance of information on this subject, but as with healthy eating, the USDA has summed exactly what you should do if you want to derive all the benefits a regular exercise program offers. You can find this information at www.healthierus.gov/dietaryguidelines.

At this Web site, you can get quick facts in an outline format about the essentials of being physically active. The core of a solid, comprehensive exercise program comes down to two key components: **aerobic training** and **resistance training.** Any regular fitness regimen should include both of these types of exercise, as each offers entirely different benefits to your body. Combined, they comprise an overall workout that will give you strength, flexibility, endurance, and cardiovascular conditioning.

Aerobic training

First, aerobic training is simply a way to improve your health through moderate-to-intense activity that increases your heart rate over a designated period of time. To promote good health, psychological well-being, a healthy body weight, and reduced risk of chronic disease in adulthood, the USDA recommends that you engage in at least thirty minutes of moderate-intensity physical activity three to five days a week. The activity you choose is up to you, but it's recommended that you choose one you enjoy. Whether it's basketball, swimming, jogging, or playing with the family dog, it's important to get your body moving by taking part in an activity that increases your heart rate above its normal resting state for at least thirty minutes.

If you want to achieve even greater health benefits, it's highly recommended that you engage in physical activity that lasts longer than thirty minutes and is more vigorous than a moderate-intensity workout. To help manage your body weight, especially as you reach adulthood, the USDA recommends at least sixty minutes of moderate-to-vigorous-intensity activity on most days of the week, while not exceeding your recommended daily food consumption.

Resistance training

To achieve the full benefits of physical exercise, you must also incorporate resistance training, the second component to a good exercise program, into your weekly exercise regimen. Resistance training helps you build strength, maintain the integrity of your bones, and improve your balance, coordination, and mobility. Overall, it allows you to keep a toned, healthy body that's more resistant to fatigue. Resistance training usually involves weights or resistance bands. You can easily do resistance training exercises in the comfort of your home. But if you like going to the gym, using machine weights or free weights are great ways to tone and strengthen muscle.

Some examples of resistance training exercises are push-ups, pull-ups, and sit-ups—all of which you can do at the gym using weights or at home using only your body. For other types of resistance-training exercises, including biceps and triceps curls, shoulder lifts, and back exercises, it's recommended that you use some weight to aid in toning your muscles and increasing your strength. A good goal to work toward is eight to twelve repetitions of six to eight strength-training exercises at least twice per week.

Warm-up

Before beginning any sort of workout, you must warm up your body. This is an absolute necessity, as neglecting it can lead to strains, sprains, soreness, and muscle fatigue. A proper warm-up involves five to ten minutes of light aerobic activity followed by stretching. If, for instance, you plan to play basketball, walking briskly for five to ten minutes, followed by stretching, is the best way to get your muscles ready for an intense game of running around the basketball court.

To stretch properly, you need to stretch each of your major muscle groups (not just the ones you plan to use), hold each stretch for at least fifteen seconds (don't bounce while stretching), and stretch to the point of mild tension (don't over-stretch to the point of pain!). And remember, stretch only after you've completed at least five to ten minutes of a light aerobic activity to get your blood flowing and your body warmed up.

When to exercise

Research has shown that people who exercise in the morning are more likely to follow through with their daily exercise regimen than are those who exercise later in the day. This is because as the day progresses, people have a tendency to get caught up in the day's activities and become tired. This often leads to a workout that either gets put off for another day or is cut short. To ensure that you remain loyal to your workout regimen, it's highly recommended that you work out early in the day. However, if an afternoon or evening workout fits your schedule better, that's fine. But be serious about your workout routine by scheduling it into your day. Remember: Exercise gives you the energy and the strength you need to accomplish your ambitious goals. By forgoing a regular exercise regimen, you decrease your body's potential to excel in life.

Exercise—a Wrap-up

We've told you about the importance of exercise and the two critical components of a healthy exercise regimen—**aerobic** and **resistance training.** Both are essential if you want to enjoy all the benefits a regular exercise program can give you. It's recommended that you do some sort of aerobic exercise at least three to five days per week, and resistance training at least two to three days per week. You can combine aerobic and resistance training in any day if you wish, or you can do them separately—it's up to you. Also, don't forget to warm up prior to exercising, as this will help prevent soreness and injury. Lastly, remember that exercise is the key to feeling better and looking better! It gives you more energy, less stress, and a much more fulfilling life.

We've now discussed two of the four principles for achieving optimal health. The third principle is to get the right amount of sleep. Like the first two principles, without this simple but critical principle, you won't be able to attain optimal well-being.

Principle #3: Get the Right Amount of Sleep

Getting enough sleep is a key to optimal health because with too little of it your quality of life will decrease in one way or another. This is because sleep is tied to everything, including mood, stress levels, alertness, weight, and the ability to digest food, perform tasks, and think clearly. An overwhelming amount of research conclusively shows a direct correlation between a lack of sleep and a negative impact on health and quality of life. Therefore, to keep your body in an optimally healthy state, it's imperative that you get the right amount of sleep. What is the right amount of sleep?

For most people, sleeping about eight hours per night is adequate. This is the amount of sleep needed to recharge and rejuvenate the body. However, some individuals may need to sleep more, while others may need to sleep less. To determine how much sleep your body needs to perform optimally each day, follow these simple rules:

- **If you wake up feeling tired, you're not getting enough sleep.**
- **If you feel sluggish during the day, despite eating the right foods and exercising regularly, you're not getting enough sleep.**
- **If you have to rely on an alternative energy source to wake up in the morning or to stay awake during the day (such as coffee or cola beverages), you're not getting enough sleep.**

A proper night's rest should give your body the energy it needs to go through the day without feeling sluggish and tired, and without feeling the need to sleep. Once you've figured how much time your body needs to renew itself each night, it's important that you reserve this amount of time for sleep. To ensure an adequate night's rest, follow these sleep tips:

- **Try to go to bed at the same time each night.**
- **Reduce or even eliminate the amount of caffeine you drink. If you have to drink caffeinated beverages, do so earlier in the day rather than later. Caffeine is a stimulant and will therefore interfere with your ability to fall asleep.**
- **Try to exercise earlier in the day instead of in the evening. If you can only exercise in the evening, do so at least three hours before you go to bed. Exercising any later than this will interfere with your ability to fall asleep.**
- **To help clear your mind, write in a journal before you go to bed.**

Your ability to be in optimal health is directly related to how much you allow your body to rejuvenate itself each night through sleeping. If you don't get the proper night's sleep, your ability to give your best each day will be compromised. Successful individuals know the importance of sleep, and therefore reserve enough time in their schedules to ensure they get the amount of sleep their bodies need for optimal performance. So, if you want to perform at your best each day, you simply must get enough sleep.

Principle #4: Engage Only in Activities that Promote a Positive and Healthy Lifestyle

You have the choice each day to do as you wish. Though parents, teachers, and friends may give you advice, what you ultimately decide to do with each day of your life lies only with you. No one is going to be with you every minute of the day to help you make the choices that will lead you to a healthy, happy, and prosperous future. You need to be in complete control of your life each step of the way, because if you aren't, you leave yourself vulnerable to chance and circumstances. You'll "float on a breeze," letting life happen to you at random rather than being the director of your life.

Each day brings new opportunities and experiences, and the decisions you make each day ultimately shape your future — for better or for worse.

It is in your moments of decision that your destiny is shaped.

— Anthony Robbins

It's important that you weigh every action you take each day for the potential benefit or cost it will have on your life. To live a happy, healthy, and prosperous life, you need to engage only in activities that will promote these qualities now and in the future. What activities do we suggest?

We suggest activities that you feel will be fun and exciting, but that won't be destructive to you or others in any way. Any activity that makes you feel good is recommended. Obviously this varies from person to person, but some great examples are going to the beach, watching your favorite TV show, playing sports, reading, playing a musical instrument, or spending quality time with your family. Choose any positive activities that will improve your life.

It's also important to engage in rest-and-relaxation activities that allow you to take time off from hard work on school-related tasks, rejuvenate yourself, and enjoy everything life has to offer. If you constantly engage only in school-related work without giving yourself proper rest and relaxation, you'll become intellectually, emotionally, and physically drained. To recharge yourself adequately, you need to take time off from work activities to relax and enjoy life.

We've discussed positive activities that will allow you to refill "the well" of your body. But we haven't mentioned anything about activities that are destructive to your body and to your future.

Activities That Are Destructive To Your Body and Future

Any activity that will cause your body to break down in any way, that will interfere with your ability to reach your school and life goals, or that's harmful in any way to others is an activity that will have a negative impact on your life. Obvious examples include the use of illicit drugs and tobacco products. These have been linked to many diseases and to behaviors that lead to impaired judgment, poor concentration, and self-destructive behaviors. There are so many negative attributes associated with illicit drugs and tobacco products that to choose to use any of these is simply a waste of your time and life. Just spend an afternoon visiting a drug-rehab facility for an eye-opening experience!

Other self-destructive activities include not being honest, taking advantage of people, and not keeping your promises. The list can go on and on, but to live a happy, fulfilling, and prosperous life means to live each day as the best person you can be, without compromising your full potential and without compromising the world you live in. Live each day to your fullest potential, make a positive contribution to society, and enjoy everything that life has to offer—because living in this manner is the only way to achieve the level of happiness, success, and fulfillment that life can provide. Make choices that will allow you to reach your full potential, because choosing anything less is not being true to what you can achieve and become.

ACTION STEPS

❑ Are you drinking enough water each day to give your body the energy it needs? If not, increase your water intake. Also, if you're drinking soft drinks and other high-sugar beverages, reduce or eliminate them, and replace them with water instead.

❑ What foods do you eat each day? Are you paying attention to the different foods you eat and how healthy they are for your body? If not, start thinking about your food choices and about what it means to eat in a healthy manner. It can mean the difference between feeling sluggish and tired or feeling energized!

❑ Visit the Web site www.mypyramid.gov and become familiar with the many different healthy food choices available to you. Then, design a customized healthy eating plan by inputting some basic information about yourself at this Web site. This is easy to do, doesn't take much time, and has immense practical power to help you create healthy eating habits.

❑ To help you track and monitor your eating habits as well as help you set goals for eating in a healthy manner each day, print a Meal Tracking Worksheet found at www.mypyramid. gov.

❑ Become familiar with the Dietary Guidelines fact sheet, which gives a powerful snapshot of what healthy eating is all about.

❑ Become familiar with foods that are unhealthy. Eliminate them from your diet, or eat them sparingly.

❑ Are you exercising on a regular basis? If not, start exercising, because the benefits of a regular exercise program are overwhelming!

❑ Are you getting enough sleep each night? If not, make sure you reserve enough time for your body to rejuvenate itself through a good night of uninterrupted sleep.

❑ Are you looking after your body and engaging only in activities and habits that will keep your body healthy, alert, energized, and attractive? If not, what can you reduce or eliminate from your lifestyle, and what can you add so you can have a healthier and more successful life?

Chapter 9

EDUCATION AND MONEY

One of the most important yet misunderstood and overlooked topics is the topic of money. Money is an integral part of life; it is the currency of living, allowing you to buy everything from food and clothing to those neat little gadgets such as cell phones, PDAs, and computers. Though the meaning of life certainly isn't about money, to live a life that is balanced and one that will allow you to enjoy each day without having to be burdened by financial struggles, it is important that you learn how to manage money successfully. Far too many students underestimate the importance of basic money-management skills, and as a result, they end up broke, in debt, or worse, with a negative credit score that can take years to overcome. And it doesn't stop there!

If you learn poor money-management skills early in life, there is a high likelihood that those skills will be carried into adulthood, only with far greater consequences. The American Bar Association has estimated that nearly 90 percent of divorces during the past ten years resulted from financial difficulties. And studies by the Children's Welfare League of America have reported a direct link between financial stress and domestic abuse. Health problems have also been attributed to financial struggle. And when it comes to your education, the inability to manage money effectively can reduce your ability to perform well in school, compromising your educational goals and your lifelong dreams. The bottom line is, if you want to ensure that you'll live a balanced and healthy life, you must learn how to manage your money, because the repercussions of financial irresponsibility are very real and immensely costly.

The good news is that you're young, and learning to become financially proficient early in life will lead to enormous and profitable benefits for you now and for the rest of your life. You just need to learn the success strategies of effective money management and be motivated and dedicated enough to integrate these powerful strategies into your everyday life—starting now! The earlier you learn these strategies the better off you'll be.

The amount of money you have now, even if it's none at all, is not important. What is important is learning the strategies presented in this chapter, because these strategies represent fundamental money-management principles, the same time-tested, proven principles that peak-performing financial experts and the wealthy use to not only manage their money, but to accumulate lots of it! These are the principles that are at the core of what being financially responsible is all about, and, not coincidentally, they're also at the core of what it takes to become wealthy over time.

Though this chapter is primarily about how to take care of your money responsibly, the principles will teach you both financial literacy and the basic strategies of wealth accumulation.

Most importantly, the principles will give you a financial blueprint for how to start thinking about money responsibly, because applying these principles will give you a mindset for understanding what it truly means to make money work for you. And by getting money to work for you *instead of being a slave to it*, you'll have more opportunities, more choices, and greater freedom to pursue your dreams and ambitions!

Now we introduce to you the **five foundational money-management principles** that have been responsible for creating financial independence and freedom for millions of individuals. These principles may seem simple, but you must not underestimate the powerful and life-changing capabilities they hold: in these five simple principles lies the difference between a life filled with financial abundance and freedom or one filled with financial struggles.

As always, the choice lies only with you to take control of your financial destiny and to create the type of life you envision for yourself. Ask yourself now, "If these five principles have worked for hundreds of years to create financial freedom for millions of people, then why can't they work for me?"

Why not?

Principle #1: Decide to Take Control of Your Financial Future

When you decide to take control of your financial future, a powerful thing happens: you allow your mind to open up to all the different possibilities for how money can become a valuable asset in your life rather than an unpleasant liability. Too many students are in debt, have irresponsible spending habits, and don't understand the basics of money management. They don't really think about money—they just spend! As a result, their financial irresponsibility leads to lives that become imbalanced and even overwhelmed by financial worries.

Many students do not know that negative financial habits learned early in life contribute to a lifelong pattern of fiscal negligence, which leads to their lives becoming enslaved by money. Instead of developing financial habits that give them the freedom and financial resources to live a life they envision for themselves, they end up living paycheck to paycheck. By deciding early in life that you want to take control of your financial future, you take the first step toward financial responsibility, and more importantly, financial freedom.

The first step to taking charge of your financial future, then, is to *make the conscious decision to do so*. It all begins with the desire and commitment to learn how to manage money responsibly. Many students never take the first step toward understanding the basics of managing money—never fully realizing that to live a balanced life, it's essential to put basic money-management principles into practice. Simply by incorporating foundational money-management principles into your life, especially at an early age, you set the stage for creating a financially healthy future.

However, to be successful and realistic in taking charge of your financial future, it's important to set aside any preconceived notions you may have of what it means to be "financially healthy." The media tends to portray those who are "financially healthy" as living exorbitant lifestyles consisting of expensive homes, high-end cars, and extravagant vacations. While this type of lifestyle can appear exciting and attractive, it's characteristic of only a small percentage of the population; it doesn't represent what's typical and what it generally means to live in a financially healthy manner. This type of lifestyle is generally associated with overindulgence, careless spending, high-profile living, and short-term gratification—all of which are not reflective of the money-management principles presented in this chapter. So set aside your preconceived notions of what it means to be "financially healthy," and open your mind to the principles we share with you in this chapter—beginning with this first principle—*decide to take control of your financial future*.

Decide now to take control of your financial future, because only after you make this decision will your mind open up to a new way of thinking about money—a way that will bring security, fulfillment, and financial abundance. And remember, to succeed in any endeavor in life you must have a game plan. It's no different with your financial future. Take the first step to developing your game plan for your financial future by making the choice to do so!

Principle #2: Get a Status Report of Your Financial Situation

Now that you've made the decision to take control of your financial future, what's next? The next step for taking control of your financial future is to get a status report of your current financial situation. What does this mean? It simply means figuring out how much money you have, how much money you have coming in, and how much money you have going out.

Many students don't take the time to figure out their financial situation, and as a result they fall prey to irresponsibility, neglect, and financial carelessness when it comes to dealing with money. They never give any thought to the money that flows into and out of their lives, and more importantly, how they can leverage this money to their advantage.

Taking responsibility for your money begins with getting a financial picture of your life. This allows you to better understand exactly what you're doing with the money that comes into your life. And more importantly, it allows you to assess your financial patterns and habits and what you may need to do to get yourself on a financially healthy path. It may surprise you to know just how much you can learn from taking a look at your financial picture.

How Much Money Do You Have?

The first part of understanding your financial picture is to know how much money you have. This is important because it gives you a starting point, a baseline, for managing your money now and in the future. At this point, it doesn't matter whether you only have a small amount of money or none at all. What's important is that you develop a mindset that will allow you to manage money in an effective and healthy way so that you can create a financially successful life.

Add up all the money you have right now — including the pennies. Break open the piggy bank, look in the desk or closet where you keep your money, and check your savings account. For those of you who don't have a net worth yet, don't worry — just go through the motions as if you had some money saved. Again, it doesn't have to be much — even $10 or $20 is okay. If you have less than this, that's okay too. Combine all your money from all the different places, add it up, and then write down your *total financial worth*.

Great! You've just determined a very important number. This number represents your financial net worth. It's an important number because it allows you to track your progress each week, month, and year to see how your net worth changes (hopefully for the better). It creates a baseline so that you can continually monitor your financial progress.

This number also gives you an idea of where you are presently in your financial life and where you envision yourself to be in the future. This will help motivate you to become financially responsible. It will help you to not spend carelessly because you are monitoring your financial situation carefully and responsibly. This is why it's important for you to find out exactly how much money you have right now and then write this number down.

After figuring out your total financial worth, it is then important to know how much money you have coming in.

How Much Money Do You Have Coming In?

What is your income? Do you have a full-time or part-time job, an allowance from your parents, or have you perhaps even started your own business? Maybe you have no source of income yet. The important point is that you determine your total monthly income, write this number on a sheet of paper, and label it "Income Sheet." Again, it doesn't matter if you have no income yet. What's important is that you learn the money-management principles presented in this chapter.

The "income sheet" you create will allow you to monitor your source(s) of income as well as track how your income changes over time. Generally, the older you are, the more sources of income you'll have. These may be from your job, interest from investments including stocks, bonds, and savings accounts, and possibly income from investment ventures you may decide to pursue. But at this point, you may just have one or two sources of income—from a job and/or an allowance from your parents. Whatever income source you have, write it down on your income sheet and then, at the end of each month, update your income sheet again with the new income. Finally, at the end of the year, fill out a report charting your yearly income.

Keeping track of your income each month and year will allow you to track how much money you bring in versus how much money you wish to accumulate over time. But more importantly, it will allow you to track your income versus your expenses. This is critical to know because this is where most students get into trouble: their expenses outweigh their income.

This brings us to the third important point for getting a status report of your financial situation: *how much money do you have going out?*

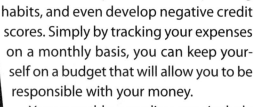

How Much Money Do You Have Going Out?

This part of your financial situation is probably the single most important component to creating a financially healthy lifestyle. Many students pay no attention to their daily, weekly, and monthly expenses, and as a result they get into trouble by getting into debt, being late on payments because they don't have money to cover their spending habits, and even develop negative credit scores. Simply by tracking your expenses on a monthly basis, you can keep yourself on a budget that will allow you to be responsible with your money.

Your monthly spending may include buying clothes and food, paying your cell-phone bill, and paying for entertainment. Add up all of your expenses and write them down on a sheet of paper that you label "Expense Sheet." This sheet will allow you to see where you spend all your money each month. It will also help you start thinking about how you spend your money and whether you're buying items that might be unnecessary.

By comparing your "Expense Sheet" with your "Income Sheet," you can easily track your monthly expenses versus income. This will help keep you on a responsible budget because you can easily compare how much money you have coming in with how much you have going out. Learning where you're spending money is a crucial component to managing your money and creating a balanced budget. It's also crucial to keeping your life in balance.

There are several computer programs that can help you keep track of your financial life. We recommend Quicken and Microsoft Money, which are great for organizing your finances, keeping track of how much money you have and what you spend, and giving you easy "snapshots" of your financial picture at any given time.

Overall, Principle #2, **Get a status report of your financial situation**, allows you to understand your financial situation more clearly and encourages you to think about the dynamics of the money in your life. How is money coming into your life, where is it going, and how much do you presently have? More importantly, it allows you to understand your patterns of spending in relation to your income.

By reviewing this financial information, you'll have a better understanding of how you can manage your money more effectively. Could you be spending your money in better ways? Could you be saving your money instead of spending it on unnecessary items? What about being more cost-effective and practical when spending?

Though principle #2 may seem simple, it has immense practical power for creating a financially healthy life. Not paying attention to how the money in your life flows into and out of your hands is similar to not paying attention to your health. Both will result in a life that becomes out of balance and not in harmony with a lifestyle that is healthy, productive, and successful.

Now that you're familiar with your financial picture, it's important to understand more specifically how you can take charge of your financial future. What strategies can you implement right now to create a foundation on which to build a successful and abundant financial life? There are key strategies that, if followed, will allow you to create and maintain a financially healthy life now and as you get older. What are these strategies? Let's find out! And keep in mind, you're about to learn the success strategies of the financially savvy and wealthy.

Principle #3: Strategies for Creating a Financially Healthy Life

Strategy #1: Keep a portion of everything you earn

It's no secret that to gain financial abundance over time, all you have to do is save. It's actually quite a simple matter, yet it's the downfall of so many people. They just don't have the discipline to set aside a portion of their earnings. Had they done so, especially beginning at an early age, they would have set themselves up for financial abundance and, more importantly, financial freedom later in life.

I found the road to wealth when I decided that
a part of all I earned was mine to keep.

— George S. Clason

Keeping a portion of everything you earn is your ticket to financial abundance. But how much should you save? Obviously, the more you save, the faster your money will grow. However, saving money should be done in a realistic way. A good target is to save 10 percent of your earnings. According to the US Department of Commerce, the average American saves well below 5 percent of what he or she earns. This usually doesn't allow for financial freedom later in life. In comparison, American millionaires save between 15 and 20 percent of their income, while those who can meet a minimum that will allow for a healthy financial future save between 10 and 15 percent. A great mark to strive for is to *save at least 10 percent of your earnings*.

If saving is something new for you, start by saving only 2–3 percent of your earnings. Then, over the course of a few months or a year, try saving up to 10 percent. And when you become more financially savvy, you can try to increase this percentage even more.

Strategy #2: Make your money work for you!

When you save money, you must make that money work for you. The days of shoving your money under a mattress, hoarding it in your closet, or storing it in a piggy bank are long gone. If you're not saving your money where it can earn a *return*, then you're not saving wisely.

What is a return? A *return* is simply money you earn by storing your money in a location where it can earn interest. You can store your money in a number of different financial investments, and in return, you'll be given money for doing so. Simply, this is free money that you'll get just for storing your money! These investments include savings accounts, bonds, money market accounts, CDs, and stocks. Notice that your piggy bank or closet is not one of them.

The Different Types of Investments

Savings Accounts
Bonds
Money Market Accounts
CDs
Stocks

An example of a typical investment would be to put, say, $500 in a savings account and let it collect interest at a rate of 5%. Over the course of a year, you'll have earned $25 for doing nothing but letting your money be stored in a savings account. Obviously, the more you invest the bigger your return. If your initial investment was $5,000, for instance, and it earned interest at 5% for a year, then you'd have earned $250 of free money. This is why it's so important that you choose now to store your hard-earned money where you'll be given free money for doing so.

In fact, choosing to store your money at home is counterproductive to your future financial health for two major reasons: The first, as you've just learned, is because your money doesn't make a return; the second reason is because of inflation. The cost of living increases over time, generally by about 3 percent per year, which means that the value of your money decreases by about 3 percent per year! This is serious because it means your hard-earned dollars are losing value every day. To prevent this, you need to invest your money where it will earn more than 3 percent per year.

Other reasons to store your money in investments, including a savings account, CD, or money market account, are because your money is safe there, because you can establish a lasting relationship with a financial institution, and because you may get added perks such as checking, monthly statements to monitor the status of your money, and online banking to help you pay your bills, transfer funds, and review transactions.

In today's financial market, there's no reason not to put your money in an investment fund, though the best reason of all to invest your money is that you'll be given free money via a return for doing so.

The power of investing your money

As you've just learned, investing your money is a powerful way to make it grow. In fact, the benefits just keep getting better. The minimum 10 percent that we're asking you to try to save might not be much now, but as you graduate from school and start earning a lot more money, this 10 percent can potentially be huge. How much? Let's review.

Look at a typical American salary of $50,000 per year. If 10 percent of this salary—about $416 per month—is saved each year over the duration of thirty-five years, this will eventually generate a huge chunk of cash. How much? A whopping $1,678,293! That's nearly 2 million dollars! And of course if more than 10 percent is saved, the numbers would be even more staggering.

You may be wondering how saving just 10 percent of a $50,000 salary each year for thirty-five years add up to a savings of $1,678,293. The answer is because of the power of a magical phenomenon known as *compound interest*.

Compound interest

Einstein called compound interest "the greatest mathematical discovery of all time." Compound interest is the interest you earn on the amount you initially invested *plus* any interest that has accumulated over time. Put another way, as your money compounds over time, you make money on both the initial investment and also on the interest on the interest, and on and on over time. As a result, your money can really grow!

Consider the following example. Let's say you put just $100 a month into an investment that earns 10 percent, and you do this for forty years. The total amount you invested would then be $48,000. But because of compound interest, your money would grow to a staggering $637,678—close to thirteen times your initial investment! And if your investment returns at an average rate of 12 percent over a duration of forty years, your money would then grow to $1,188,242—nearly twenty-five times your initial investment! This is the beauty of compound interest—your money just keeps growing at a significant rate the longer you let it grow.

We've shown you a rate of return based on *compound interest*. But there's another type of interest called *simple interest*. The difference between simple and compound interest is that simple interest is calculated based only on the initial dollar amount, whereas compound interest keeps compounding continuously over time.

Consider the following example. If you invest $5,000 at a rate of 10 percent over a ten-year period using *simple interest*, you'll earn $10,000 for your investment. If you invest this same amount using compound interest instead, you'll then earn $12,968. You'll have made an extra $2,968 simply because of compound interest. Obviously, compound interest is the way to go, because you can earn much more money in an investment based on compound interest rather than simple interest.

See another example of compound interest in the chart below.

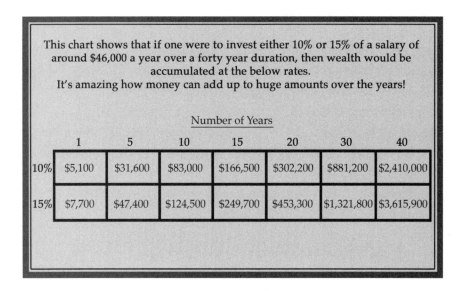

This chart shows that if one were to invest either 10% or 15% of a salary of around $46,000 a year over a forty year duration, then wealth would be accumulated at the below rates.
It's amazing how money can add up to huge amounts over the years!

				Number of Years			
	1	5	10	15	20	30	40
10%	$5,100	$31,600	$83,000	$166,500	$302,200	$881,200	$2,410,000
15%	$7,700	$47,400	$124,500	$249,700	$453,300	$1,321,800	$3,615,900

Always look for investments that are compounded, and keep in mind the more money that is compounded, the faster and larger it will grow. Financial institutions can choose to compound money daily, monthly, quarterly, or yearly, so try to find investments that compound in the shortest amount of time.

The psychology of building your nest egg

As you start saving, you'll start building a nest egg. At first it may not seem like much and it may grow slowly, but over time, as you become more diligent and responsible with saving your money, it will start growing faster. It is important that you be aware that much of saving money and building a nest egg comes down to not only the physical part of saving, but also the psychological part.

The most powerful way to encourage new money to come into your life and to keep building upon the money you've saved is to continually watch the current money you save grow over time. As you watch it grow, this will actually motivate you to keep saving even more. This is why it is important for you to be responsible about keeping your nest egg growing and to not dip into it impulsively to buy any item that's not a necessity.

This becomes even more critical as your nest egg grows large enough to accommodate those more expensive and exciting purchases that come within your financial grasp. However, you must resist these nonessential purchases because they will destroy your nest egg, compromise your ability to manage money effectively, and most importantly, compromise your ability to gain financial freedom.

Strategy #3: Control your expenditures

The last strategy for creating a financially healthy life is to control your expenditures. It won't matter how much money you earn or how much you save if you don't control your expenditures. Spending more money than you earn will only create a life of financial slavery, not one of long-lasting abundance and financial freedom.

> *The only way to create long-lasting wealth is to bring in*
> *more than you spend or spend less than you bring in!*
> — Sandy Forster, international best-selling author

It's imperative that you create a financial lifestyle that is faithful to responsible spending. Most people believe that the secret to financial abundance is to find ways to earn more money. This isn't entirely accurate, because generally the more people make, the more they spend. They get caught up in a vicious cycle, trying to make more money only to spend more, so they never get ahead in life, but succumb to financial slavery and end up living paycheck to paycheck.

The Small Purchases

The downside of spending isn't the large purchases, but the many small, everyday purchases that people get caught up in making. It's the continuous buying of all those little things each day that end up costing a lot. Most people think carefully before purchasing any big-ticket items, but when it comes to buying those small-ticket items, they give no thought to how this will affect their overall financial picture. Over the long haul, casual purchases such as soda, chips, coffee, fast food and magazines, for example, can cost a fortune.

Let's take a look at how spending just $5 or $10 a day on unnecessary expenditures can add up to a lot of money.

$5/day spent over a week = $35. This is approx. $150/month.
If this amount was invested and earned
a 10% annual return, you would make:

1 year	=	$1,885
2 years	=	$3,967
5 years	=	$11,616
10 years	=	$30,727
15 years	=	$62,171
30 years	=	$339,073
40 years	=	$948,611

Spending $10/day over a week = $70. This is approx. $300/month.
If this amount was invested and earned
a 10% annual return, you would make:

1 year	=	$3,770
2 years	=	$7,934
5 years	=	$23,231
10 years	=	$61,453
15 years	=	$124,341
30 years	=	$678,146
40 years	=	$1,897,224

As you can see, spending just $5 a day can cost $339,073 over a thirty-year period, and close to a million dollars over a forty-year period, if instead you invested $5 a day at a rate of 10 percent. And if you spend $10 a day, this can cost you $678,146 over thirty years and nearly $2 million over forty years! When you really see how those "little" expenditures add up, it's shocking.

Minimize unnecessary purchases

To keep yourself on a healthy financial plan, you need to analyze your day-to-day spending habits and figure out whether the purchases you make are really necessary. The sooner you figure out which ones are unnecessary and can be eliminated, the sooner you'll get on a path to financial health—a path that will allow you to amass a lot of money over the course of your life instead of wasting it on purchases that may add no real value to your life. As you just learned, spending just $5 a day can cost you close to a million dollars over a forty-year period. This is money that you could use to retire comfortably.

Don't spend carelessly

To develop a financially healthy life, you need to develop habits that allow you to manage your money responsibly. These habits don't require you to change much of how you live day to day; rather, making small, subtle changes will have a huge impact. The one main habit you must learn is to not spend carelessly, especially on items you don't really need or that you buy just to impress others.

Too many people spend money they haven't earned,
to buy things they don't want, to impress people they don't like.
— Will Rogers

Before you make that purchase, ask yourself these essential questions:

- **Is this expenditure really necessary?**
- **Is this an impulse purchase or a planned purchase?**
- **Is the price reasonable?**
- **Can I get something similar for less?**
- **Will I regret this purchase?**

If you can answer these questions satisfactorily before making a purchase, and you still find that the item is a necessity, go ahead and buy it. And bear in mind you don't always have to keep yourself on a strict financial regimen, buying only items that are absolutely necessary. Buying the occasional cookie or magazine might make you happy, so give yourself a break now and then, but generally try to be responsible about how you spend your money—especially on the "small" stuff.

Be responsible with credit cards

The single biggest reason students today get into so much financial trouble is because of credit cards. Credit cards are the source of serious problems including debt, bankruptcy, divorce, lost dreams, health problems, and emotional wreckage. What may start off innocently enough as making purchases on a little piece of plastic often ends up leading to a life of financial turmoil. This is mainly because credit cards allow the customer to make purchases with split-second ease, without much thought about handing over any "real money" in the form of cash when purchasing items. It's this convenience, simplicity, and the buy-now-pay-later mentality that makes credit cards so appealing to millions of people. Yet these same reasons, unfortunately, lead to many people's financial undoing.

How Do Credit Card Companies Make Money from You?

To understand how people get into financial trouble using credit cards, it's important to understand how credit card companies make their money from customers. The companies' main source of revenue is from the interest rates they charge customers to use their credit card. For instance, if a credit card charges an 18.5 percent annual rate to use their card, this means they charge you a rate of 18.5 percent on any balance that's unpaid at the end of each month.

That can be a lot of money! Let's look at exactly how much.

Take, for example, a cardholder with a balance of $2,500 and an annual percentage rate of 18.5 percent. If he or she paid only a minimum amount each month, equivalent to about 2 percent of the total balance, then it would take over thirty years to pay off the balance. Even worse is that a total of $6,500 in interest charges would have accrued during this time on that initial balance of only $2,500. This is why it's so important to try to pay off your balance each month. The credit card companies allow a "minimum balance" not for your benefit, but for theirs. They don't want you to pay off the entire balance because if you do they won't make any money from you.

So, the main way credit card companies make money from their customers is by charging them interest on balances that aren't paid off in full at the end of each month. Other ways they make money are by charging late fees, charging an annual rate to use their cards, and through cash-advance charges. So when you're looking to apply for a credit card, shop around for the best deal just as you would with a ste-reo system or car.

Below are the three key factors to consider when reviewing poten-tial credit card deals.

Interest rate: Always look for the lowest-interest credit card. Inter-est rates can vary, but generally any rate higher than 14 percent is not considered good. Get the lowest rate you can, as this can save you a lot of money.

Annual fee: Many credit card companies charge a flat annual fee just for you to have their card, whether you use it or not. But if you do your research, you can easily find a credit card with no annual fee.

Grace period: This is the period that a credit card company may give you to make your monthly payment before they consider the payment late. Obviously, the longer the grace period, the more flexibility you have with your monthly payments. Some credit card companies don't offer a grace period. It's to your benefit to find one that offers as long a grace period as possible, so you can save money by avoiding late fees.

Overall, when using a credit card you must understand that this is not a magic card that can make all your dream purchases come true. Realize that every time you use your credit card to make a purchase, no matter how small, you're going into debt. Don't fool yourself into thinking that you have more money than you actually have and buy items you can't afford. Every time you go into debt using your credit card, you dig yourself deeper into a financial hole that gets harder and harder to get out of.

Debt only brings with it financial slavery, and financial slavery limits your options for success and happiness in life. The more debt you have, the harder it is to succeed and be happy. Choose to take responsibil-ity for your financial future, and develop the habit of using your credit cards only in a mature and responsible manner.

Here are guidelines that you can follow to help you use your credit card responsibly:

- Figure out in advance how much credit card debt you can afford to pay back each month, and don't spend a dollar over that amount!

- Use the twenty-four-hour rule. Wait twenty-four hours before you make any purchase on a credit card. This gives you time to consider the intended purchase and whether you really need the item. It also allows you to find out whether you can get the item cheaper elsewhere.

- Limit the number of credit cards you own (two is more than enough).

- Always make your payments on time, and whenever possible, pay off your balance in full. If you can't, then pay the maximum amount you can.

- Never use your credit card to withdraw cash—there are high finance charges for this.

- Review your monthly statement and report any questionable charges to your credit card company immediately.

- Never lend your credit card to anyone.

- Keep your credit card in a safe place.

- Know the terms of the credit card contract before signing it.

Credit cards can be a great convenience because they provide simplicity and a buy-now-pay-later benefit for you. A credit card gives you great purchasing power, but it can also lead to financial instability in your life. Therefore, before deciding to use a credit card, make sure you feel confident that you'll use it responsibly and in a financially healthy manner. If you have any doubt, then wait until you feel you can handle the responsibility, because the financial repercussions of credit card neglect are very real and costly.

Your FICO Score

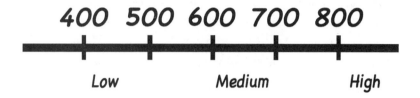

FICO SCORE RANGE

Now that we've discussed credit cards, let's discuss a very important term, "FICO score," and its crucial role in your financial health.

What is a FICO score? Your FICO score is a number based on five factors:

- **Outstanding debt—including credit card debt and car or house debt.**
- **Past payment history (late payments, delinquencies, and bankruptcies)—the fewer late payments the better.**
- **How long you've had credit—the longer you've been building a credit history the higher your FICO score.**
- **New applications for credit—opening too many accounts in a short time can negatively affect your FICO score.**
- **Types of credit—including credit cards, car loans, and mortgages you currently have.**

All five factors combine to give you a number that represents how "credit worthy" you are to lenders. Whether you can get a credit card or a loan to help buy a car, house, or any other item (including a stereo system, computer, or TV) is greatly determined by your FICO score. The higher your FICO score, the more "credit worthy" you are to potential lenders—which means the easier it will be to borrow money from them. That's why it's crucial to be aware of all the factors that affect your FICO score and do what's necessary to keep it as high as possible.

We've now given you **three principles for creating a financially healthy life**: *decide to take control of your financial future; get a status report of your financial situation;* and *strategies for creating a financially healthy life*. However, there are additional ways you can ensure a financially healthy life. In fact most people who attain great financial security and success do so through endeavors that take their earning potential to the next level. What are these endeavors? Let's find out!

Principle #4: Take Your Earning Potential to the Next Level!

By following principles 1, 2, and 3, you'll put yourself on a path to financial health. But only principle #4 can help you grow your nest egg faster and with greater potential. In fact, most millionaires make their money not by the first three principles, but through following this next one, which consists of three different wealth-building strategies.

The successful wealth builders find additional ways
to add to their growing nest egg.

— Richard Paul Evans

Wealth-building Strategy #1:
The Power of Investments

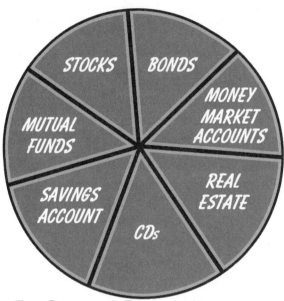

THE DIFFERENT TYPES OF INVESTMENTS

We showed you how you can earn free money by putting your money in investment vehicles such as stocks, bonds, CDs, savings accounts, and money market accounts. But we haven't yet shown you how certain investment vehicles have the potential to far outperform others. Each type of investment has its advantages and disadvantages for each particular situation, and it's important that you understand the basics of the different types available to you. This will allow you to make important informed decisions about which investment vehicles will be right for you as your financial situation grows and matures over time.

Another reason it's important to understand how investments can accelerate your earning potential is because if you don't invest your hard-earned money, over time it actually loses value due to inflation. So it's critical to the health of your financial future that you learn how to invest your money as soon as possible, especially early in your life. This will allow you to create a mindset that will keep you on a path of financial success now and as you get older.

The various types of financial investments

Savings Accounts

Opening a savings account is a great way to start investing your money. It allows you to become familiar with how banks operate, and to start investing your money in a safe, secure, and easy way. One of the great advantages of opening a savings account is that, compared with many other investments, it requires only a small amount of money. For students, who often have very little money, this is an ideal way to start investing.

Another advantage of savings accounts is the flexibility and ease of adding and withdrawing money. Savings accounts are "liquid," which means you can deposit or withdraw money at any time without penalty (unless, in some instances, you fall below a minimum-balance requirement). They are also FDIC-insured, which means that if for any reason the bank goes out of business, the federal government will pay back your money up to $100,000. Another advantage is that interest is usually compounded daily instead of monthly or quarterly, as in other types of investments, which means your money grows faster. And lastly, some savings accounts give you the flexibility and ease of managing your money online.

Realize, however, that savings accounts aren't high-return investments. A typical savings account offers yearly returns of only 0.2–0.40 percent, though with proper research, you can find returns of 1–3 percent and in some instances around 5 percent. A great resource for checking competitive rates of savings accounts is www.bankrate.com, or read the *Wall Street Journal* or *Investors Business Daily*, which also give up-to-date information on the varying savings account rates available. Other disadvantages of some savings accounts are monthly maintenance fees, and penalties for letting your balance fall below a certain amount. Therefore, thoroughly research the many different savings accounts available to ensure that you find the best offer.

Overall, savings accounts offer a number of advantages that other investments don't, but use them cautiously because they're low-return investments. Many investment experts reserve savings accounts as temporary "garages" in which to park their funds while they seek higher-paying investments. It is also good to keep funds in a savings account for day-to-day activity and for emergencies. How you choose to take advantage of the benefits of a savings account is up to you. The important point to understand is that a savings account is an investment vehicle that offers unique advantages that other investments cannot.

Money Market Accounts

Money market accounts are a great alternative to savings accounts for those who want to set aside some money and earn a higher rate of return. Similar to savings accounts, money market accounts are simple to understand and are extremely secure. When you invest in a money market account, you're actually investing your money in liquid securities—these are short-term government bonds or highly rated corporate bonds. Other advantages of money market accounts include being FDIC-insured, the ability to withdraw funds, and in some instances, a "tiered" rate of return. This means that as your balance grows the rate of return increases.

A major disadvantage of money market accounts is that your money is usually not as "liquid" as in a typical savings account. This means you can't withdraw funds as readily as you would from a savings account without being penalized for doing so. Usually, you're only allowed a minimal number of withdrawals per month before a penalty is assessed. Another disadvantage is that opening a money market account often requires a larger minimum balance than opening a savings account. Monthly maintenance fees may also be assessed, and these can add up.

Overall, a money market account can be a great alternative to a savings account. You just need to be fully aware of the advantages and disadvantages before deciding to put your money into this type of investment vehicle.

Certificate of Deposit (CD)

Certificates of deposit are another great alternative to savings accounts because they offer a higher rate of return and are safe investments. With CDs, you're usually required to invest a minimum amount (usually at least $1,000) for a period of three months to five years. In return for storing your money with them, banking institutions will give you a higher return than a savings account or money market account because you agree in advance to not touch your money for the duration of the CD. Typically, the longer the length of the CD the higher the interest rate that's offered. And like savings and money market accounts, CDs are generally FDIC-insured to protect your investment.

A major disadvantage of CDs is that you can't access your money until the term of the CD is complete. Choosing to withdraw any portion of your money earlier will result in fees being assessed, as well as a possible reduction of the interest rate. Therefore, when choosing a CD, it's wise to make sure you won't need quick access to any of the money you plan to invest.

Overall, CDs are great investments that offer interest rates above those of savings and money market accounts. Before committing to a CD, though, you need to be fully aware of the benefits and the drawbacks, and make sure this type of investment is right for you.

Bonds

A bond is simply a loan to a government or company in exchange for repayment of the initial investment plus interest. When you invest in bonds, you're lending your money to the government or a corporation in exchange for being paid a return. Why do they want to borrow money from you? The government might need to raise money to build highways or bridges, for instance. Corporations need your money to expand their business operations or to develop a new product. As a result, you can benefit from their needs by lending your money to them and getting a reasonable return for your help.

Similar to CDs, bonds have a specific period of time—anywhere from a few months to thirty years. This means that your money will be inaccessible for the duration of the loan (unless you want to get penalized for withdrawing it early). Bonds differ from CDs because they pay interest at set intervals. A bond investment may pay interest monthly, quarterly, or semiannually, so you don't have to wait until the loan term is complete to get paid a portion of your return—it happens periodically.

Another benefit of bonds is that they're considered a very safe investment. Investing in government bonds will guarantee a return, and investing in high-rated corporate bonds is considered safe, unless, of course, the company goes out of business.

Bonds can also provide tax benefits. For government-issued bonds, any interest that's earned may be tax-exempt. This benefit can add up to a lot of money over time.

Overall, bonds are a great investment vehicle for many reasons, so it's to your advantage to consider this type of investment and decide if it's right for you. Though the typical return on bonds is higher than on savings accounts, it pales in comparison to the potential return you can earn on our next type of financial investment—stocks.

Stocks

A stock is actually a tiny piece of ownership in a company. When buying stock, you buy a piece of a company. When the company does well, the value of its stock usually increases, which means more money for you. If, however, a company performs poorly, this may negatively affect its stock, and you may lose money. Stocks are also known as "equity" or "shares."

Unlike the other types of investments, stocks come with no guarantees for how they will perform. They can go up or down at any given time, for any reason. This makes stocks one of the riskiest types of investment vehicles in which to invest your hard-earned money. So why do people invest in the stock market?

Stocks offer returns that can far surpass any of the other investments we've mentioned. You can earn returns of 10 to 20 percent or more—even double or triple your initial investment over a relatively short period of time. However, you can also lose this amount of money. That's why you should invest in the stock market with caution and only with money that you won't need for emergencies or everyday expenses.

You can minimize your risk in the stock market by choosing to invest in low-risk stocks. These are "blue-chip" stocks, which represent well-established, conservative types of companies such as IBM, Ford, and Microsoft. With low-risk stocks, however, there's usually a smaller return compared to high-risk stocks.

High-risk stocks offer the promise of great returns, but they're considered risky because they usually represent startup companies. With any new company that hasn't built an established track record, it's hard to predict whether the company will succeed, how successful it will become, or whether it will fail and soon go out of business.

The general rule with investing in the stock market is that the safer the investment you choose, the lower the return, and the riskier the stock, the higher the potential return, but also the higher the potential for loss. It's up to you to invest your money in a way that's comfortable for you. With any stock investment, always do your research, consult with a financial expert if necessary, and invest only the amount of money that, if lost, will not affect the quality of your life.

To help reduce the risk of a stock-market investment, many financial experts say that it's best to invest in several or many different stocks simultaneously. This ensures that if one stock fails, returns from the others will help stabilize your loss. You can invest in multiple stocks through mutual funds, which are a combination of stocks overseen by a fund manager (mutual funds can also be a combination of stocks, bonds, CDs, and money market accounts).

Mutual Funds

Mutual funds are a great alternative to investing in individual stocks. Their value generally doesn't fluctuate as rapidly or to the extent that individual stock prices do, so they provide a level of security that investing in one stock can't offer. Also, mutual funds are professionally managed by knowledgeable fund managers. This means that someone is looking out for your investment even when you may not be.

Generally, mutual funds return at a much higher rate than savings accounts and bonds. Therefore, investing in a mutual fund is something you should consider if you're looking for a relatively safe investment that has the potential to return at a good rate. But be careful — keep in mind that mutual funds usually represent large collections of stocks and as such have the potential to lose value.

One of the main advantages of mutual funds is that they allow an investor to invest in a well-diversified portfolio of stocks, bonds, CDs, and money market accounts with only a small amount of money (as little as $100). So, what normally would require an investment of thousands of dollars costs only a fraction of that when you invest in a mutual fund. Yet the investor can still take advantage of all of the benefits (and losses) associated with investing in many different types of investment vehicles.

Overall, mutual funds are a great way to invest your money, especially if you want the comfort and security that investing in a diverse portfolio offers. It allows you to not have to risk your money investing in individual stocks, which sometimes fluctuate greatly in price. Therefore, your risk is not as high, but you still have the potential to earn a good return (especially when compared to savings accounts and bonds). It's to your advantage to consider the unique benefits a mutual fund can offer when you're looking at higher-return investment vehicles.

Asset Allocation

Asset allocation simply refers to how financial investments are divided. Many financial experts believe that dividing money into many different investment vehicles—stocks, bonds, mutual funds, money market accounts, and real estate—is the best strategy for protecting the overall investment. Spreading money over different types of investments has the potential to vastly reduce the overall risk. An example of an asset allocation is 50 percent of your investment in CDs and bonds, 35 percent in stocks, and 15 percent in cash (savings account). Factors usually considered when choosing how to invest money are personal goals, level of risk tolerance, investment objectives, and the age of the investor.

For risk tolerance, the higher the acceptable level of risk, the more money is put into investment vehicles such as stocks and mutual funds. The less risk one wants the more money is invested in vehicles such as CDs and bonds.

Regarding age, the older you get, the less risk you should take. This is because if you lose money on a risky investment when you're young, you have plenty of time to recoup your losses. As you get older, though, you have less time to recoup your losses. Also, responsibilities increase, such as supporting a family and making mortgage and/or car payments. Therefore, financial experts agree that when investing, it's wise to diversify your money into age-appropriate types of vehicles.

Overall, asset allocation is a great way to protect your investment portfolio. It allows you to invest in many different vehicles with the assurance that if something bad happens to one of them, the others will help compensate for the loss. Therefore, asset allocation is something you should consider when investing money, especially as you become more financially successful.

We've now covered wealth-building strategy #1, the power of investing. To get more information on investing, check out these Web sites, which provide great practical advice.

- www.younginvestor.com
- www.beginnersinvest.about.com
- www.amateurinvestor.org
- www.teenanalyst.com
- www.investopedia.com

We now move on to the next wealth-building strategy and show you how you can continue to take your earning potential to the next level through the many work-related opportunities available to you.

Wealth-building Strategy #2: The Power of Increasing Your Earning Potential through Work-Related Opportunities

Learning the value of earning money through work is an important step in maturing and developing the skills necessary to make you successful. Even if you're fortunate enough to have parents who'll support you during your education, it's important that you learn the value of earning your own money early in life. This will allow you to develop characteristics consistent with being a healthy, well-rounded, and self-sufficient individual—one who's capable of living independently. Also, it will help you understand the responsibility, hard work, and commitment that go into earning your own money. This wealth-building strategy will show you how to increase your earning potential by taking advantage of the limitless work-related opportunities around you.

Those who achieve prosperity are the ones who develop the mind-set of looking for opportunity in everything they do. They constantly look for ways to increase their growing nest eggs, and as a result are able to create a financially healthy life. It should be no different for students. By learning early in life how to increase your earning potential through work-related opportunities, you'll get on a financially healthy path right away.

There are many ways to increase your earning potential. As you start looking for them, you'll find an abundance of work-related opportunities that surround you that you may not have thought of or even noticed before. What are these opportunities? Let's take a look at them.

The best places to start looking for work-related opportunities are in activities you truly enjoy. That is, do what you love and get paid for it!

Believe me, when you are doing something you
absolutely love and you're making money at the same time —
it really doesn't get any better than that.

— Sandy Forster

Your work-related activities should not interfere with your school obligations. School should always be your first priority. Now let's look at potential jobs that can be fun, exciting, and a great way to increase your earning potential.

- Tutor other students if you enjoy a certain subject or if you just enjoy teaching.
- Be a lifeguard or give swimming lessons if you enjoy going to the beach or pool.
- Baby-sit if you enjoy being around kids.
- Design a Web site for others, or fix computers, if you're good with computers.
- Be a medical/dental assistant if you find these fields interesting.
- Pet-sit if you enjoy animals.
- Cook meals for elderly persons if you like cooking (or you can just help out around the house).
- Be a team coach or assistant coach for a youth sports team if you love sports.
- Be an assistant to a lawyer if law fascinates you.
- Help with gardening if you like growing flowers and vegetables.
- Help with a drama/theatrical production if you enjoy acting or singing.

- **Get certified and teach aerobics or weightlifting if you enjoy the gym.**
- **Be a photographer if you like taking pictures.**

Other jobs may include:

- **Be a host or waiter/waitress at a restaurant.**
- **Wash windows.**
- **Clean houses or office buildings.**
- **Wash and wax cars and boats.**
- **Put up and take down Christmas lights (seasonal work opportunities).**

The list can go on and on. There are unlimited possibilities for increasing your earning potential. Just put your mind to work thinking about what you love to do and then create an income stream from it.

As you get older, of course, the quality and types of opportunities to earn will change and evolve. For instance, while you're a student, you may choose to increase your earning potential by tutoring other students. But as you get older, you might choose to start your own business educating others — like we did! Our passion was to help other students do better in their educational journey, and as a result, we didn't look far to create a job opportunity from our passion.

However, if you enjoy a field such as medicine or dentistry, then you can assist in a medical or dental office to help you prepare to become a physician or dentist. Or if you enjoy designing Web sites or fixing computers, you can use these skills to help you become a cutting-edge Web-site designer/computer programmer. Do you like law? Then a job helping lawyers at a law office will help you prepare to become an attorney. The possibilities are endless!

The point is that there are many different opportunities for you to increase your earning potential. Just look at your interests and then put those interests to work, have fun, and make money doing what you love to do!

Wealth-building Strategy #3:
The Power of Home Ownership

Owning a home may seem like something that's far off in the future, but it's important that you realize home ownership is one of the best financial investments you can make. It has been shown for decades that owning a home is one of the most reliable and profitable investments.

Nothing you will ever do in your lifetime is likely to make you as much money as buying a home and living in it.

— David Bach

It's important to understand the benefits of home ownership, and how you can start preparing mentally and financially for your first home. But keep in mind, you don't have to start saving for that big house on the hill—begin by saving for a "starter home" such as a small condo or townhouse. This is the best way to think about your first home, since it's a more realistic and attainable short-term goal.

As they start college, most students will rent because they don't have the financial resources to buy a home. That's perfectly okay, but as soon as you're financially able, it's best to stop renting and start owning.

Why is home ownership so important and such a powerful way to build wealth? Because by renting, you're throwing away money each year, but when you own a home, you're continuously earning money from the potential increased equity value of the home.

Here's a simple but powerful example to show you why owning a home is far superior to renting. Let's say you rent an apartment, condo, or home at a price of $1,500 per month and you rent it for thirty years. However, the landlord increases the rent by 5 percent each year (which can be expected). At thirty years, you'll have paid close to $1.2 million to your landlord—and have *nothing* to show for it! In comparison, if you own a home that you bought for $200,000 and paid a $1,500 monthly mortgage payment for thirty years, at the end of that time you'll not only own the home free and clear, but you'll own a home that's worth a lot of money. How much? If the value of your home increased by 6 percent each year during the thirty years you made mortgage payments, your home would now be worth $1.1 million! Can you see why owning a home is far superior to renting?

But the benefits just keep getting better. According to the Federal Reserve, the average homeowner in America is worth more than thirty-four times as much as the average renter. Also, homeowners are able to get great tax breaks that renters can't. These can add up to thousands of dollars. Also, by owning a home, you're not subject to rent hikes or the possibility of eviction. And lastly, owning a home gives you pride of ownership and a piece of the American dream. You'll have a sense of accomplishment, happiness, and security knowing that the place you live in is all yours.

The bottom line is that owning a home is one of the best financial decisions you can make—one that has the potential to make you lots of money over the years. It's then to your advantage to start thinking about home ownership right away. Set aside a little bit of money each month if you can. Your savings will add up, and eventually you'll be able to make the leap and buy that starter home you've been dreaming of.

Keep in mind that the current statistics show that more people than ever under the age of twenty-five are buying homes. Why not you?

To help you prepare for your first home, the Web sites below are great resources for first-time home buyers. Start taking action now to prepare yourself mentally and financially to own a piece of the American dream!

- **www.hud.gov**
- **www.ncsha.org**
- **www.fanniemae.com**
- **www.freddiemac.com**

Principle #5: Give Back

> *We make a living by what we earn —*
> *we make a life by what we give.*
>
> — Winston Churchill

This chapter has focused on teaching you how to live a financially healthy life, an important skill in this complex modern society. However, it's not the most important skill or the most important goal. The point that Churchill made is that the true measure of our success is not what we earn, but what we do with what we have.

The world places enormous importance on the ornaments of life. Some people will form their good opinion of us because we have the right clothes, cars, toys, and other material items. These are life's ornaments, not life itself. Good people and history will judge us not by our material possessions, but by what we did with our lives and our talents, and how we helped make the world a better place.

You might be tempted to say, "I'll get around to helping others when I'm old and rich." You might think that because you don't have great wealth, the call to give back right now doesn't apply to you. Nothing could be further from the truth.

You already have great wealth! Your time, talent, love, goodness, and youth are great treasures. The world is in need of you right now. You can become a student philanthropist. You don't have to wait to promote good and improve the quality of life of others.

Perhaps this is a tough time for you and you find yourself just barely hanging in there because of school, work, and family obligations. If you feel "down and out," you might wonder if you really have anything to offer. Believe it or not, this could be one of the best times for you to help others. Most people find that by helping others, they help themselves. Psychologists have long suggested that volunteering is a great way to lift yourself out of a down mood. Volunteering brings light and life to others as well as to you.

Mother Theresa, winner of the Nobel Peace Prize, said, "Let us not be satisfied with just giving money. Money is not enough, money can be got, but they need your hearts to love them. So spread your love everywhere you go."

And you don't have to go far to do this. The opportunity to help is right where you live. Maybe a friend needs encouragement, or a fellow student could use some tutoring in a difficult subject. The school would benefit from your volunteering to reach out to those in need in the community. Stop by to visit an elderly relative and give the support of your love and youth. These are but a few examples. The point is that you already possess a golden treasure that can help make the world a better place. It's you! Even donating just a little bit of your time, perhaps an hour every week or two, can make a huge difference in someone's life.

We've all heard about the incredible generosity of Bill and Melinda Gates, Warren Buffet, and Oprah Winfrey, to name just a few. You can join their ranks right now. Become a student philanthropist and help make the world a better place by simply… *giving back*.

ACTION STEPS

❑ Have you made the decision to take control of your financial future? Are you being responsible with how you manage your money? Make the choice now to learn how to manage money in a healthy and responsible manner.

❑ Do you know your current financial situation? What is your financial net worth? How much money do you earn and how much do you spend each month? Figure out these numbers because they'll allow you to understand your financial habits and patterns for spending in relation to your income.

❑ Are you keeping a portion of everything you earn? If not, try to save a minimum of 10 percent of what you earn. If this is too much, then start with 2–5 percent, and gradually increase this amount to 10 percent.

❑ Are you in control of your spending? Do you watch what you buy each day, especially the low-cost and unnecessary items that over time can add up to a lot. Monitor how you spend your money, and before you buy it, think about whether an item is really necessary.

❑ Are you responsible with your credit card(s)? What is the interest rate? What are the late fees and cash advance charges? Become familiar with the terms and conditions of your credit card agreement(s) because this familiarity can save you a lot of money.

❑ Do you know your FICO score? Become familiar with this score and those factors that can increase or decrease it. To find out your FICO score and to further understand what it means, go to www.FreeCreditReport.com.

❏ Do you know the difference between a savings account, money market account, CD, and bond? How about stocks and mutual funds? Become familiar with these different types of investments, and start investing as soon as you can. Realize that the earlier you start investing, the better off you will be.

❏ How can you increase your earning potential? Think about different jobs that interest you and learn more about them. Then take action and get involved in a job that you feel will be fun and exciting. There is no better feeling than getting paid for what you enjoy doing!

❏ Start thinking about how you can mentally and financially prepare for your first home. Owning a home may seem far off to you, but realize that you can take small steps now to help you become financially capable of owning a home in the future.

❏ Give back by donating your time to help others. There are many people who need assistance in one way or another. Make the world a better place by giving back.

Chapter 10

PERSONAL DEVELOPMENT

You are living in a time that is more abundant, more prosperous, and more filled with opportunities than ever before in history. Never has it been so easy to accomplish goals and to succeed in life than it is in current times. The advent of technological advancements such as the information superhighway, power-notebook computers, cell phones, and digital micro-software capabilities have made students' lives easier, more efficient, and able to accomplish much more in a shorter period of time. At no time in history have so many resources and opportunities been available to succeed in life.

With the future looking so bright, it's only logical to ask the simple question, "Why are some students using the abundance of available resources and opportunities to create a better future for themselves while others are not?" What is it about those successful students that enables them to make the choices, seek the opportunities, and use the available resources to create fulfilling and prosperous lives while other students make poor choices and engage in activities that lead to unfulfilling and unsuccessful lives? Furthermore, if we are living in a society of abundance and opportunity, why do only a small percentage of students reach their full educational potential? Why don't all students take advantage of this great time in history to reach their full educational potential?

The answer to this simple question is why this chapter is perhaps the most important and consequential in this entire book. If we could tell you the reason why one student succeeds while another fails, despite similar social, economic, and family backgrounds, we would in essence be giving you the formula for success in accomplishing your educational goals. More importantly, we would be giving you the very mindset it takes to succeed not only in accomplishing your educational goals, but also in accomplishing any lifelong endeavor that you set your mind to.

This is because there are certain **laws of success** that are so powerful, so effective, and so universal, that when applied to any endeavor in life, they are guaranteed to give enormous and lasting results. In fact, these are not only the laws that star students apply when setting out to accomplish their educational goals, but the same laws that practically every successful businessman, doctor, lawyer, author, politician, and celebrity has used to achieve their extraordinary level of success. People like Oprah Winfrey, Bill Gates, Steven Spielberg, J. K. Rowling, and former President Bill Clinton, among many others, have used these foundational laws of success to achieve their goals. It's an undeniable reality that these laws are responsible for producing some of the most influential, powerful, and respected people in all of history.

Bill Gates

Steven Spielberg

Oprah Winfrey

So what are these laws of success? This final and most profound chapter of this book is devoted to revealing these laws, why they're so critically important to apply in pursuit of your educational goals, and exactly how you can start implementing them in your everyday life right now.

But first, it's important to realize that in order to make these laws work in your life, you need to apply them with passion, sincerity, and unwavering conviction, because if you let them, these fundamental laws of success will change your life forever!

The Laws of Success

Law #1: The Law of Belief

The law of belief states that whatever you believe with feeling and conviction will become your reality. Simply stated, you are what you believe. If you believe you'll be successful, and you believe it passionately, then you'll become successful—but if you believe you won't, it's most certain that you won't.

> *Whether you think you can or you can't,*
> *either way you are right.*
>
> — Henry Ford

This simple law is so powerful that if you expect to succeed in your education, it's imperative you believe passionately that there's no other outcome than that you will succeed. And the degree to which you believe it is the degree to which it will come true. It's a simple fact of life that the more we believe in an idea, goal, or vision, the more it will manifest itself into our lives. For this reason, it is crucial that you believe in yourself—in the attributes that will allow you to develop into a successful, healthy, and goal-oriented individual. You must exclude any destructive, self-limiting beliefs you have about yourself from your belief system, because they'll only prevent you from reaching your full potential.

For the law of belief to work, however, you must be absolutely clear and specific about the beliefs that you wish to enter into your reality. If, for instance, you desire to earn high grades, it is not enough to simply desire them.

BE SPECIFIC AND CLEAR ABOUT THE FUTURE YOU WANT TO CREATE.

You must be specific and clear in how you envision yourself earning those grades. In fact, the more descriptive and clear you are, the more able you'll be to reach your goal. You must, for example, be specific and realistic about the time you'll have to study, the office hours you may need to attend, and the detailed class notes you'll need to take. Then once you firmly believe that you're capable of earning high grades, and are realistic about what it will take to earn them, you'll be much more likely to do so — by the law of belief.

This is a simple but very powerful law that is effective, proven, and capable of changing your life in more ways than you can imagine. The mere fact that you believe you are able to achieve something, and you believe it passionately, will set into motion actions that will bring into your life the circumstances and events that will allow your beliefs to become reality. This works extremely well — if you let it. It's the secret that star students use to achieve extraordinary success, and it's the secret that virtually all successful people in history have used to achieve their goals. The bottom line is that once you *believe* in yourself and your capabilities, the possibilities for success are endless!

Law #2: The Law of Attraction

The law of attraction simply states that, like a magnet, you will attract into your life the people, circumstances, events, ideas, and opportunities that harmonize with your dominant thoughts, especially those that bring forth strong emotions.

Like any force of nature, your thoughts carry with them great potential to bring forth changes in your life that are direct reflections of what you most think about. And it is these thought-driven changes that eventually shape your reality. Simply put, *your thoughts determine your reality*.

> *All that we are is the result of what we have thought.*
>
> — Buddha

If you want to be successful in life, and in particular your education, it's essential to think only those thoughts that are consistent with success. This means keeping your thoughts focused on what it will take for you to reach your goals. If, for instance, one of your educational goals is to earn higher grades, think only those thoughts that will allow you to achieve this goal. Any thoughts that are counterproductive or in any way not in harmony with achieving this goal should be excluded from your daily thought process. Ask yourself only the questions that will help bring what you want into your life.

For example, if you're earning C grades in your classes, don't ask, "Why do I keep earning Cs?" By asking this type of question, your mind will give you answers to why you earn Cs, instead of allowing you to focus on how you can earn higher grades. You need to ask yourself better questions, such as "How can I earn higher grades?" Only then will you get better results.

This is a simple but very powerful and effective strategy that successful people use to reach their goals—they keep their thoughts focused only on those factors that will allow them to reach their goals, while excluding any thoughts that won't. In essence, successful individuals continuously filter their thoughts, allowing only those that are in harmony with their visions of becoming successful. They don't allow their minds to be cluttered with thoughts that could deter them from achieving their goals.

It's essential to realize that your thoughts are the foundation to your reality and that what you think about is what you invite into your reality—for better or for worse. This is why it's imperative to keep your thoughts focused only on those attributes you wish to attract into your life. If you want to be successful, you must continuously think only thoughts that will bring you closer to success. And then your thoughts will attract the people, circumstances, ideas, opportunities, and resources into your life that will ultimately allow you to succeed!

Law #3: The Law of Expectation

Our lives are shaped not so much by our experiences
as by our expectations.

— George Bernard Shaw

The third important law, the law of expectation, states that whatever you expect with certainty becomes your self-fulfilling destiny. If you expect good things to happen, they usually will. On the contrary, if you expect bad things to happen, then the outcome will generally be negative. You continuously set the stage for how your life will unfold by predicting how you feel the events in your life will turn out. When you talk about these events, your expectations determine your attitude toward those events, and your attitude greatly influences how those events will unfold.

Truly successful individuals think and speak positively about events and circumstances, and expect the best outcomes to occur. And by the law of expectation, they are seldom disappointed. This is yet another secret of the truly successful. They expect only the very best in their lives, and as a result their lives are filled with more abundance, happiness, and success than are those who don't live lives of positive self-expectancy.

Regarding your education, expect that you'll earn high grades, that you'll have the confidence and the ability to run a school organization, or that you'll be elected to a position in student government. By expecting only positive outcomes in your life, you'll create an environment that favors the outcome you desire. Because by being an optimistic person, you create an environment filled with confidence, happiness, and excitement, and this will allow you to become more energized and motivated to achieve your goals. Also, people will be attracted to you, and by this attraction, the people around you will be inspired by you and will be motivated to help you achieve your goals.

Overall, creating a life of positive expectancy allows you to create your future. It allows you to approach every situation with confidence, determination, and optimism, no matter what you may be experiencing in your life. You'll see even momentary setbacks as learning experiences that will enable you to progress toward your goals with even greater strength. Having this mindset will enable you to move forward toward your goals with the expectation that you have the ability to accomplish any goal you set your mind to!

Law #4: Have a Positive Attitude

One of the most important keys to living a life filled with happiness, achievement, and prosperity is to live each day with a *positive mental*

tal attitude. Your ability to succeed in every area of your life, including your education, directly correlates with the attitude you project toward the people, events, and circumstances that are part of your everyday experiences. No other personal characteristic leads to more accomplishments, more triumphs, and more personal satisfaction than having a positive attitude in your everyday life.

Attitude is a little thing that makes a big difference.

— Winston Churchill

In fact, the simple characteristic of having a positive attitude is one of the *key reasons* why some individuals are able to gain more financial wealth, prestige, and recognition than those individuals who rely on aptitude or ability alone. It's really that important! In fact, a positive attitude is such a critical component for success that without it, you're virtually guaranteed to struggle in attaining any goal you set out to accomplish, including those related to your education.

The logical question then arises, "What is it about a positive attitude that makes it such a valuable component to success in life?" To answer this question, one has to look no further than understanding the basic psychology of the relationship between two people. The characteristics of a positive attitude — optimism, cheerfulness, and enthusiasm — are the same characteristics of people who are well liked and respected. And it is for these reasons that these individuals become attractive to others causing people to gravitate toward them.

It then becomes simple to understand how much easier it is for people with positive attitudes to reach their goals and to succeed in life than it is for people who don't. Individuals who are constantly negative, unhappy, and complaining are the ones who find themselves with the fewest friends, the fewest opportunities, and the least success. The most direct path to accomplishing your educational and lifelong goals is to always try to maintain an optimistic and enthusiastic outlook on life, no matter what the situation.

Being positive in your every day interactions with the people and toward the circumstances that you encounter is the best way to ensure you will lead a life that is fulfilling, rewarding, and immensely successful. It is also the surest way to accomplish any goal you set your mind to!

Law #5: The Importance of Goal-setting

If you want to be a peak performer and want to achieve the dreams you envision, you must get into the simple but very powerful habit of goal-setting. It's a proven fact that by setting clear, specific, and time-dependent goals, you greatly increase your chances of accomplishing those goals. Thinking and talking about your goals isn't enough to set into motion the actions necessary to achieve them. Only by articulating your goals in detail, and setting specific timelines in which to accomplish them, can you create an effective game plan. And once you're clear about what it will take to achieve your goals, you'll be much more focused and determined to do so.

Study after study has shown that those who set goals, especially written goals, have a vastly greater chance of achieving them than those who don't. In fact, less than 5 percent of people ever bother to set goals, and less than 1 percent write their goals down. And not coincidentally, this is the same small but very elite group who are the peak-performing individuals of our society. It's then an amazing fact of reality that if you engage in the simple act of goal-setting, and if you're really serious and committed to doing so, you'll be well on your way to joining this elite group!

To set goals that will work, you must know how to set effective goals. How do you do this? First, you must set goals that are consistent with what you truly desire. Setting goals that aren't in harmony with your passions in life will only lead to a compromised performance and a lack of motivation to achieve those goals. But if you set goals that are consistent with what you're truly passionate about, then your drive to achieve them will be unsurpassed.

The second rule for effective goal-setting is to set goals that are realistic and believable. This means setting goals that might be a stretch for you to achieve, but that you believe you can attain with enough hard work and persistence. By stretching yourself, you may have to set goals that will take you out of your comfort zone and require you to push yourself more than you may be used to.

And lastly, it means setting many smaller, short-term goals that will allow you to ultimately achieve your greater, long-term ambitions. If, for instance, you desire to attend law school, it's unrealistic for you to make that a long-term goal if you don't set short-term goals to perform well in your classes. However, if you set small short-term goals to maintain a specific grade-point average, then your long-term goal of attending law school will become much more attainable.

Effective goal-setting also means that you must write your goals down. Research has shown that one of the most important factors in goal-setting is to have clearly defined goals that are *written down*. You can accomplish much more if you see your goals on paper than if you just carry them around in your head. And the more specific, detailed, and clear you are in your plan to reach your goals, the more likely you are to accomplish them.

Along with having clearly defined written goals, you must also set specific deadlines by which to reach them. Setting deadlines activates your subconscious to start thinking about what it will take for you to achieve your goals. Then, once you're clear about what you'll need to do to achieve your goals, your subconscious will then set into motion the actions that you'll need to take to make your dreams become reality.

The last factor in effective goal-setting is to have a clear plan of action. This means knowing in detail the necessary actions, along with the people whose help you'll need to achieve your goals. For example, if you plan on forming a school club, find out what administrative paperwork you'll need to complete, whom you'll need to contact, and where and when the club will meet. You should also write down all of this information, and set specific deadlines in which to reach each goal. Again, the more detailed and clear you are about your goals, the more likely you'll achieve them.

Finally, don't feel that your plan of action to reach your goals has to be set in stone. In fact, the best way to achieve your goals is to continually revise your plan as new ideas arise and more effective strategies become apparent. The bottom line is that you must have a plan for each goal you set for yourself.

If you fail to plan, you plan to fail.
— Anonymous

Goal-setting is truly a powerful and life-altering habit, and it has the potential to radically change your life for the better. Goal-setting is simple, takes little time out of your schedule, and is something you can start immediately! The research is clear on the enormous benefits of goal-setting. If you want to accomplish your ambitions and dreams in life, it's important to realize that goal-setting is one of the surest and quickest ways to achieve them.

Law #6: The Power of Association

It's no mystery that the people we surround ourselves with shape us as individuals. Every person you choose to associate with influences the way you think and act. The way you think about your life, how you act toward and react to the people and circumstances you encounter each day, how you set goals and spend your time, and most importantly, who you strive to be, is greatly influenced by the people you surround yourself with. This is why it's critical that you surround yourself with people who are success-minded, who think positively, and who have high ambitions in life. Choosing to associate with people who have no ambitions, who are always negative and pessimistic, and who are going nowhere in life is the surest and fastest way to join them.

In fact, it's been shown that if you teach someone the foundational principles of success (believing in oneself, thinking positively, setting effective goals, etc.), and put this individual in a group of people who have no ambitions in life and don't follow any success principles, this alone is enough to prevent that person from succeeding.

Hanging out with people who accept mediocrity or, worse, engage in self-destructive habits, is enough to prevent you from achieving your goals. This also applies to your education: if you choose to hang out with students who earn poor grades, don't take part in extracurricular activities, and don't take school seriously, your school performance will be negatively affected.

Birds of a feather flock together

If you want to succeed in school, it's essential to associate with students who are serious about school and about their future. It's as simple as that.

You need to view the world not only as a place with unlimited opportunities, but also as a place that is a reflection of who you are as a person. The person you choose to be each day and who you strive to become is reflected by the people with whom you choose to associate. If you want to be serious about your education and about your life, it is essential that you use the **power of association** to associate with those people and circumstances that are consistent with being successful!

Law #7: Never, Ever, Give Up!

The last law of the success mindset is to never, ever, give up in the pursuit of your dreams. You can look at any successful person in history and it is an absolute certainty that they overcame setbacks and obstacles. In fact, failure is an inevitable part of the success formula. With any worthwhile goal or ambition, you must realize that to succeed you can expect to experience failure. Some of the greatest success stories in history were preceded by some of the worst failures.

> *Most great people have attained their greatest success*
> *just one step beyond their greatest failure.*
>
> — Napoleon Hill

The only real difference between winners and losers is that the winners keep picking themselves up after experiencing defeat and continue pushing forward toward their goals, while the losers just give up. Those who choose to be successful choose to persevere through setbacks and obstacles because they know that success is theirs for the taking if they just try hard enough.

Don't view failure as shameful or discouraging; actually, failure can be one of your greatest assets. Through failure you become wiser, more confident, and stronger in character—and, of course, that much closer to success.

To succeed in achieving your goals you must never see any obstacle as too difficult or impossible. View every obstacle as a learning experience and as something you can overcome with enough persistence and hard work. Part of the strategy of overcoming setbacks and obstacles is to identify them before you encounter them—because once you've identified them, they become much easier to deal with.

In relation to your educational goals, it's important to realize that it's not the momentary defeats that make the real difference in your educational journey, it's the ultimate accomplishment of achieving your goals. They're yours for the taking if you just work hard enough, stay determined and focused, and have a never-give-up attitude!

The Wrap-up!

You've now been presented with seven of the most influential and powerful laws in history. With these laws, you've been given the mindset that some of the most successful and influential people in the world have used to create their extraordinary lives and achieve incredible levels of success.

It is through these laws that what seems impossible becomes reality. More importantly, through these laws you are given the ability to break through any self-limiting belief you may have and unlock your full potential—not only in your education, but also in any endeavor you set your mind to in life.

The choice is yours. Your destiny lies in your hands to do with your life as you choose. Take control of your life and future, and create the life you envision!

Go confidently in the direction of your dreams!
Live the life you've imagined.
— Henry David Thoreau

ACTION STEPS

❑ What do you really believe about yourself? Do you believe that you will reach your educational goals and be successful and happy in life? Realize that what you believe about yourself has enormous influence on how your life will unfold. Therefore, believe in those attributes that will allow you to develop into a successful, well-adjusted, and happy individual.

❑ What people, circumstances, events, ideas, and opportunities are you attracting into your life right now? Are they consistent with the type of person you want to be and the educational goals you want to achieve? If not, what changes can you make now to begin living the life that you envision for yourself?

❑ Do you always expect that good things will happen in your life, or do you live each day with a pessimistic attitude? Realize that your expectations for how events and circumstance will turn out have a direct affect on their outcome. Therefore, always expect the best for your life!

❑ Do you have a positive attitude in life? Having a positive attitude is such a critical component for success in life that without it you are virtually guaranteed to struggle in attaining any goal you set out to accomplish, including those related to your education. Maintain a positive attitude in your life and watch how much easier it will be to attain your goals.

❑ Set clear and specific goals for accomplishing your desires and ambitions in both your educational pursuits and in your lifelong endeavors. Set specific deadlines by which to reach these goals. Then devise a clear plan of action that will allow you to accomplish them.

❑ Whom do you associate with on a daily basis? Do your friends support you? Are they a positive influence on your life? Realize that whom you associate with greatly influences the way you think and act. If necessary, change whom you associate with to create a more positive and successful environment for yourself.

❑ Do you have a never-give-up attitude in pursuit of your dreams? Realize that failure is an inevitable part of the success formula, and it is only by persevering through setbacks and obstacles that success will be yours for the taking!

We shall never cease from exploration
And the end of all our exploring
Will be to arrive where we started
And know the place for the first time.

— T. S. Eliot

About the Authors

Twin brothers Brian and Jeff Haig founded Maximize Your Education to help students become as successful as possible in their educational journey. Their mission is to empower, inspire, and provide the tools and skills necessary for your educational success.

Jeff Haig received his BA from the University of California, Los Angeles, his MBA from the University of Southern California, and is completing his doctorate in education on scholarship at the University of Southern California. Jeff is passionate about education and making a positive difference in students' lives. In college, he founded and led many organizations and clubs, was a member of a #1 debate team in the country, and mentored and tutored students of all backgrounds. Jeff has taught students at both the domestic and international level working for top educational companies and schools. He is currently a college instructor, an author, and a consultant.

Dr. Brian Haig has a BA in neuroscience from the University of California, Berkeley, where he graduated at the top of his class. He completed his doctoral studies at the University of California, Los Angeles. He has founded organizations that have significantly helped students reach their full potential, and has developed audio programs and seminars that have positively impacted the way students view their role in their education.

www.MaximizeYourEducation.com

Index

P lease visit our Web site at **www.MaximizeYourEducation.com** for additional products and services including audio programs, high school and college consulting, and our free newsletter.